ENTREPRENEUR ENLIGHTENMENT

A Guide to Establishing Your
Purpose-Driven Business

Irina Mihaela, BSc, PEng

BALBOA.PRESS

A DIVISION OF HAY HOUSE

Balboa Press books may be ordered through booksellers or by contacting:

Balboa Press
A Division of Hay House
1663 Liberty Drive
Bloomington, IN 47403
www.balboapress.com
844-682-1282

Print information available on the last page.

ISBN: 978-1-9822-0607-9 (sc)
ISBN: 978-1-9822-0608-6 (e)

Balboa Press rev. date: 03/22/2022

To all my clients who have asked questions and given me the opportunity to teach what I have learned.

* * *

To you, because you dare to be different, have the desire to follow your purpose, and are in service to humanity.

CONTENTS

PART 1

The Inner Workings of a Purpose-Driven Business

PART 2

The Outer Workings of a Purpose-Driven Business

INTRODUCTION

Congratulations on picking up this book and wanting to learn how to establish your purpose-driven business by becoming an enlightened entrepreneur.

I believe purpose-driven entrepreneurs have an important mission: to make the world a more peaceful and loving place. And you are one of them. You will learn how to combine practical business strategies with spiritual principles so that your business thrives and you can stay committed to your purpose.

The Story of How This Book Came to Life

I have wanted to write a book for years. I was focusing on writing my memoir with lessons of empowerment derived from my life's story. The memoir proved to be a difficult book to write because of all the emotions related to remembering the hardships I endured in my childhood. Another impediment was my inability to sit alone in front of the computer night after night. While I enjoy writing and have kept journals since I was in elementary school, typing for hours is not appealing to me.

On the other hand, I can spend days teaching, interacting, and answering questions. I love sharing my knowledge with people. Over the years I've been teaching the Entrepreneur Enlightenment principles to my clients, but writing them all down in a book was not on my radar. The Universe had another plan and cleverly tricked me into bringing this book to you. I'll give you the full story so you can appreciate the magic of this book showing up in your hands today.

The story starts with a scary incident: our big sheepdog bit my former husband's arm in three different places. He needed to be taken to the emergency room to get stitches while I spent the whole day with the police and animal control trying to capture the dog. This event put me into an emotional spin and I booked a session with my intuitive healer to bring myself back into a balanced state.

During the session, the intuitive healer said that I needed to dig deeper into my spirituality. I was surprised. I told him that I already pray, I meditate, I draw oracle cards, I journal, and I teach spirituality. I felt I was already doing everything I could to connect with my spirituality. He told me that I had to start collaborating with the Universe at a much deeper level.

After that session I sat down and prayed intensely. I said something like this: "Universe, if you want me to collaborate with you, send me something that will blow my socks off. Send me something that I will know for sure is a miracle. You know I teach spirituality. I need to know this firsthand; I need to know for sure if there is a path I should take. I need to know if there is a purpose, and if you are behind all this."

A few days later, on November 11, I got a phone call from a radio show executive producer. He said they thought I would make a good radio show host and asked me if I would be interested. Of course! I said yes right away. I was so excited. When I asked how he found me, he told me that they have researchers who comb the internet for people who are professional and interesting, and who have a unique message.

We sealed the contract a few days later on a full moon. The contract required eight weeks to get all the show materials ready. When we counted the weeks to see when the start date would be, we ended up with January 11. I later learned that my show's time slot was at 11:00 am.

I take the repetition of the numbers as a spiritual sign. The repetition of numbers is sometimes called angel numbers, and it is believed to be a way for the Universe to communicate messages to us. They first contacted me on 11/11 and the show began on 1/11 at 11. I knew this was my miracle; the repetition of number one made it clear that the Universe was behind me. I always knew my purpose was to share what I know with many people around the world. I just didn't know how to make it happen. The Universe did.

In the weeks that followed, I was asked to come up with a show title and description, and then to deliver the weekly shows for a duration of four months. I had been teaching my private clients about Entrepreneur Enlightenment, so I selected this name as the show's title. Every week, I'd select a topic and organize the main ideas for the show, creating about five PowerPoint slides as guidelines. Then I let myself flow during the hour-long show. I also answered questions from callers. During this time my audience grew from zero to over 6,000 people from 47 different countries, which my producer found to be outstanding. I was so excited to produce content and to have a big audience to share it all with.

Producing and marketing the show added to my already busy schedule. At the same time I was coaching at the Academy and with my private clients, hosting and facilitating events, and taking a course. I felt as if I was running in front of a train keeping up with everything. I hired an assistant to support me with marketing the show, but I still ended up feeling exhausted. After the four-month initial contract, I decided to put the show on hold. It was a hard decision for me to give up something that was so popular.

On a recent session with my intuitive healer, I asked him why the radio show came to me if I had to stop it after only four months. He surmised that the radio show was just to get me started on sharing the Entrepreneur Enlightenment philosophy with the public. Now, he said, it was time for me to write and spread the teachings.

So here I am, writing. Luckily, I have the radio show transcripts to start me off.

How this Book is Organized

My intention with this book is to show you how to combine traditional business principles with spirituality and love so both you and your business thrive.

I believe that when you follow your purpose, you do not struggle and you do not just survive—you thrive.

Part 1: The Inner Workings of a Purpose-Driven Business

This part is about what you need to do before you take your business out into the world.

We start with defining enlightenment, defining entrepreneurship, and discovering the connection between the two.

You will learn how to set up your business to match your purpose, and this will position you for success. This part will be most valuable to people who are new to business; however, more advanced business owners will also benefit by tweaking a few aspects of their approach to align their business with their purpose.

Some of my clients already had a successful business before learning these principles. Some were exhausted working long hours, and some were stuck at a certain level of income and were looking for new ways to grow.

I remember one client in particular who didn't actually want to grow her business; all she wanted was to have a little more of a life. When we integrated her purpose into her business, she found more relief, more joy, and more flow. She rediscovered her passion and was ready to grow again.

Part 2: The Outer Workings of a Purpose-Driven Business

This part is about how to take your business out into the world.

This is where you will learn about how to love marketing, how to release the fears of receiving money for your services, how to price your services right, why packaging your services is important, and how to make the sale with love.

Engaging in marketing and sales is the best way to test your enlightenment because this is when your ego and fears show up the most. When we are in our ego, we usually fear rejection. We don't want to tell people about what we do.

Fear of rejection will limit your marketing efforts and will make you want to hide. We will explore how you can overcome the fear of rejection and how you can run your business from a loving point of view. After all, doing business by loving your clients is a great way to fulfill your purpose and thrive.

During a sales conversation your fears may come up even stronger. In the marketing phase you talk with many people and inform them about your services or products. However, at the sales stage, you have to actually talk with one person, face to face, and ask for their business. In other words, you have to ask for money. This is much harder to do because the ego is afraid that you may not be good enough; that you may not know enough. Many entrepreneurs feel shy when asking for the sale. What you will learn in Part 2 will help you transcend your fears and lead you to a thriving business.

The best way is to read a chapter at a time, understand the Entrepreneur Enlightenment concepts presented, and then tweak your business to implement what you learned. Mastering one chapter per week will cause your business to grow, and your soul to be fulfilled.

I envision you applying the concepts with ease. It is my intention that you get a lot of value out of it. My style is to teach in simple terms. At times you might think you know those principles but nothing is actually really understood until it is implemented. Only then will you see how the concepts work for you. I believe that you can thrive in business while following your purpose and this book will help you do so.

In this journey of entrepreneurship, you will become enlightened.

> *"It isn't by getting out of the world that we become enlightened, but by getting into the world...by getting so tuned in that we can ride the waves of our existence and never get tossed because we become the waves." Ken Kesey*

Entrepreneurship can toss you. Learn to ride the waves. Become the waves and find your path to enlightenment and abundance.

Take my hand and let's go!

PART 1

THE INNER WORKINGS OF A PURPOSE-DRIVEN BUSINESS

CHAPTER 1

The Enlightenment and Entrepreneurship Connection

Let's start by exploring how enlightenment and entrepreneurship are connected. Some believe that these two elements are not only separate but mutually exclusive. You either choose renunciation–going without–if you are on the spiritual path, or you choose the action-oriented accumulation of goods if you are on the business path. I will explain how business and spirituality are in fact closely linked, and how your life and work gain more meaning and magic when you run a purpose-driven business.

Enlightenment Defined

Here are the two main dictionary definitions of enlightenment:
1. Enlightenment is the final destination of one's spiritual evolution; the final stage reached in the Buddhist and Hindu religions when one no longer suffers or feels desire, and they are at peace with the universe.
2. Enlightenment is the state of understanding something clearly.

The first definition says that enlightenment is a final destination. I disagree. I believe that enlightenment is a state of being, and we can be in a state of enlightenment whenever we transcend our ego and our fears. We can be in a state of enlightenment many times a day on most days. We are in a state of enlightenment whenever we focus our attention on love rather than fear; whenever we respond from our higher consciousness rather than our ego. As we progress on our spiritual path, our aim is to increase the amount of time we are in an enlightened state.

The first definition also says that to be enlightened, you need to feel no desire. Here I disagree again (to a certain extent). I believe that being in an enlightened state means that you are content with what you have in the present moment; that you are in a state of appreciation of what is. On the other hand, I also believe that we are here in the physical plane to create new things and to expand our world. Desiring to get to the next level of business is part of what I understand as expansion. In order to expand your business, you have to learn to transcend your ego and your fears, which then brings you to a state of enlightenment.

If I had no desire to reach more people, I would not be typing out this book now. Maybe having no desire works for monks who dedicate their life to meditation and praying, but for the rest of us, desire is what keeps us going. Having no desire in my opinion can lead to depression. I find it elating to create, to find ways to grow, and to see the expansion.

Trying to get rid of desire is what keeps many spiritual entrepreneurs stuck or financially unstable. They think it is not spiritual to desire financial wealth. They have great difficulty charging money for their services, which in turn makes it hard for them to stay committed to their life's work. Some find themselves forced to go work for others, sometimes in a job that doesn't fulfill them.

Through my work with entrepreneurs, I have discovered that it is our ego that actually keeps us small. When we have no desire, we can safely stay in our comfort zone. This means, however, that we are hiding our gifts, and as a result we do not serve our purpose. When we transcend the ego, and are in an enlightened state, we are willing to share our gifts and be rewarded in exchange.

It's true that being in an enlightened state means we no longer chose to suffer. Being enlightened means that we can be at peace with the universe. It is normal to still feel pain when life throws us a curveball, but to suffer means to feel powerless in the situation. In a state of enlightenment, we understand that everything happens for a reason, and to help us progress on our spiritual path.

The second definition clarifies this further: "enlightenment is the state of understanding something clearly". This is in line with what I teach. When we're in a troubled situation, we will find the answer if we get ourselves into a state of enlightenment through meditation, prayer, or positive affirmations.

I will combine the two dictionary definitions, keeping what I've come to understand through my work to give you a basic principle that will help you proceed with the information in this book:

> *Enlightenment is a state of understanding life clearly: when we demonstrate spiritual evolution and choose to no longer suffer, and when we are at peace with the Universe.*

Entrepreneurship Defined

I found a few different dictionary definitions for entrepreneurship:
1. Entrepreneurship is the activity of setting up a business or businesses, taking on financial risks in the hope of profit.
2. Entrepreneur is someone who exercises initiative by organizing a venture to take benefit of an opportunity and, as the decision maker, decides what, how, and how much of a good or service will be produced.

In *Business Dictionary*, according to economist Joseph Alois Schumpeter, entrepreneurs are not necessarily motivated by profit but regard it as a standard for measuring achievement or success. Schumpeter discovered that entrepreneurs greatly value self-reliance, strive for distinction through excellence, are highly optimistic, and always favor challenges of medium risk.

I believe there is a distinction between a purpose-driven entrepreneur and someone who just has a business. An entrepreneur is a free-spirit, someone who wants to make their own mark in the world by providing services or creating products in their own unique way. They follow a calling–their purpose–taking risks and making the unknown known, making something out of nothing. They are not motivated by profit; they are motivated by purpose, growth, and contribution.

The person who is in it just for the money is motivated by profit and makes decisions to minimize risk. They tend to follow proven business models for success. They choose to operate franchises or a business where the calculations on paper show a potential for monetary gain.

This of course is a simplistic way to look at the topic. The aim of this book is to show you a clear understanding of how business and spirituality go hand in hand, and to teach that it is possible to make money while also fulfilling your purpose.

You can see why entrepreneurs are better positioned for enlightenment; they follow a desire inside of them–a dream, a calling– and are willing to take risks to achieve their vision. They listen first to their calling and then to reason. They are willing to follow their purpose no matter what. Those are the innovators and the people who make a unique contribution to the world. Does this describe you?

> *When we align our business with our purpose, it becomes easy to pursue both spiritual growth and business success.*

How to Become an Enlightened Entrepreneur

I've created a definition of enlightenment specifically for entrepreneurs. It has three important parts.

Being in a state of enlightenment means you:

1. Have transcended your ego and your fears,
2. Fully accept that you are a perfect expression of the divine, and
3. Understand you come into this life with an important purpose.

The first part of this definition speaks about transcending your ego and fears. Doing so will help you take risks, take action, and move forward with what you are here to create. This also helps you respond well to life's challenges. Letting go of your ego helps you have better relationships which in turn gives you more support and energy for your purpose.

The second part refers to accepting that you are perfect, that you are divine—we all are. If you do not believe that you are good enough, that you have what it takes, then you might not even try. As a spiritual teacher, I've had to overcome my own ego: the voice that asked, "who am I to teach?". I observed that we are all completely capable of carrying out our purpose.

The third part is to know that your purpose is important, and the world will benefit by you fulfilling it. To establish your purpose-driven business, and to give it all you've got, you need to believe that you have a purpose and that fulfilling it benefits others. This will keep you going when you might be tempted to give up.

The Path to Enlightenment through Entrepreneurship

Over the years while coaching purpose-driven entrepreneurs to establish and expand their businesses, I discovered that there is a path to enlightenment through entrepreneurship. I noticed that someone's business is a very good feedback mechanism for how aligned they are with their purpose and to know if they are in a state of enlightenment.

I observed that when someone is in state of enlightenment, customers and opportunities come to them and that their business thrives. On the other hand, when they are not in an enlightened state, although they might work hard, the results are not quite what they hoped for.

When you feel that you are working hard but you're not achieving the results you expected, don't work harder. Instead, stop and ask yourself some of the following questions:

> ➢ Am I working from love or ego and fear?
> ➢ Am I more focused on my purpose or money?
> ➢ Do I feel deserving and good enough or unworthy?
> ➢ Am I taking chances, or am I limiting myself?
> ➢ Am I aligned with my path?
> ➢ Am I allowing others to support me?

As you meditate on each of those questions you can see what is true for you and you can adjust your approach. This is how your business gives you an indication of whether or not you are in a state of enlightenment and if you are aligned with your purpose. This is how business and spirituality meet.

I love working with entrepreneurs because an entrepreneur's actions—or the lack of actions—produce a result, and that result is visible in the reality of their business. When working for somebody else, one's actions have some effect on the overall business, but the direct effect is not always clear. As a result, it's harder to correct the path because the link from cause to effect is not direct. However, our own business will respond very rapidly to our energy: whether we attract clients or not, whether we attract opportunities or not, whether we see abundance coming in or not—all of this depends on our vibration.

It is harder to be a leader in your own business than a leader working for another person or in a corporate setting. In a corporate environment, you can hide behind processes and procedures, behind your boss, or even behind your staff. In your own business, there is no place to hide. If something is not working, you need to observe and adjust your alignment and your vibration.

I see the entrepreneur's path like climbing a mountain. If you come to a wall, you can stand there and cry about how it is impossible to continue, or you can look around to see an alternate route to continue your climb. Is turning back a third option? I don't think so. Giving up is rarely an option that leads to happiness. You need to look at alternatives: bring all you are to the game and use your creativity, determination, and conviction to find your path. This is how personal development and spiritual enrichment are directly linked to your business success.

If we want to thrive, we need to find ways to progress that are sustainable and fulfilling. We need to find ways that give us more energy instead of leaving us depleted. This is possible only when we work in conjunction with the Universe.

> *"There are only two symptoms of enlightenment, just two indications that a transformation is taking place within you toward a higher consciousness. The first symptom is that you stop worrying. Things don't bother you anymore. You become light-hearted and full of joy. The second symptom is that you encounter more and more meaningful coincidences in your life, more and more synchronicities. And this accelerates to the point where you actually experience the miraculous." Deepak Chopra*

CHAPTER 2

Knowing Your Purpose

I believe we all have a specific purpose in this world. We feel fulfilled, happy, and accomplished when we follow our purpose. Our lives take on more meaning when we feel aligned with our higher self, spirit, the Universe or God, or whatever name you prefer to call that greater force that makes your heart beat.

I believe everyone's ultimate purpose is love: to love who they are, to love the people around them, and to put love into the world through their work. This is the journey of life.

Clarify Your Purpose

Over the years many people have come to me to ask about their purpose. I've been told I have a gift in helping people discover what that is. I use both intuition and logic to do so. I have developed several questions to help anyone tune into their purpose.

If you're looking to find out what your purpose is, answer these questions below. Even if you know your purpose already, I encourage you to still give it a go because your purpose evolves as you are journeying towards it.

What Are Your Skills, Talents, and Experiences?

No matter where you are now in life, you have the skills you developed, the talents you were born with, and the experiences you have gained from living your life. These make you unique.

We fulfill our purpose when we express our uniqueness. If we copy or model other people, we will not really become all that we can be. We will miss the point of our authenticity. This is a real struggle because human beings have a deep desire to belong. We look for acceptance and we want to fit in. This creates a contradiction because in order for us to follow our purpose, we need to be unique and stand out.

At times you will feel weird and misunderstood. Standing in your uniqueness others might find you bizarre. Of course, we have way more things in common with others than not. We all have our human journey with all of the pain and all of the joy. You need to be willing to be different in order to follow your purpose.

Take an inventory of your skills, talents, and experiences to discover what makes you unique. Write these down.

What Are Your Recurring Challenges?

There is no life without challenges. We all have certain patterns that repeat in our life. Those are the lessons that we have come here on earth to learn.

Are there certain patterns that are not easy for you to comprehend? I believe that following your purpose gives you that desire to understand certain things, to overcome challenges, to overcome tendencies, to overcome repeating patterns, to learn the lessons, and move forward.

I have found that everyone has all the skills, talents, and experiences they need for their purpose. At the same time we all have something we need to overcome. The desire to fulfill your purpose helps us overcome recurring challenges and grow into a better person.

That yearning inside of us is daring us to grow: we want to learn and to increase our capabilities. When we combine our uniqueness with what we are here to learn we find our purpose.

When I was invited to do the radio show on VoiceAmerica.com, I had to let go of the fear of criticism. Receiving criticism is one of my recurring challenges. I encountered criticism from an early age in my family, having the feeling that I was never good enough for them.

To avoid criticism, I learned to work extra hard to ensure my work was perfect. Like many I had the false belief that if my work is flawless, then there would be nothing others could criticize me about. This was tiring and, of course, unachievable. If someone is in their ego, they will find something to criticize you for. The way forward for me was to become immune to criticism.

I don't speak English perfectly; I speak it with an accent because it is not my first language. What made it harder for me to want to be on air for the radio show was that in my culture if you don't express yourself well verbally, it is perceived that you are not educated enough. On the other hand, I knew my purpose is to talk with as many people as I can and share what I have learned about entrepreneurship. When the radio show opportunity was presented to me, I knew right away that I needed to accept it in order to fulfill my purpose, and at the same time I had to once again face my fear of criticism.

To fulfill my purpose, I had to grow myself into a person that was comfortable speaking on the radio. When my pronunciation was off I had to let go of any judgments and continue, rather than being bashful or constricted. On radio dead air is not acceptable so I could not stop just because I mispronounced a word. I had to accept my imperfections and keep going. I put myself in a challenging position because I felt a strong calling to fulfill my purpose. And you know what, every time I am in a challenging position I end up surprising myself at how well I do! You've probably experienced this too.

When I take inventory of my skills, talents, and experiences, I see that I have great presentation skills and I take great joy in sharing my knowledge. My talent is to take complex concepts and explain them in simple terms so they are easy to comprehend and apply. I also have a deep passion to help others get clarity and move forward. Plus, I have years of experience talking in front of large audiences. This makes me a perfect candidate for the radio show and the fear of criticism is only something I had to overcome.

This is an example of how we are provided with all the skills we need to fulfill our purpose. We then have the incentive to improve ourselves, to become better, to let go of our limitations, and to move forward.

> *"He who has a WHY to live can bear almost any HOW."*
> *Friedrich Nietzsche*

This is why committing yourself to your purpose is so important. The purpose is the "why," and for fulfilling your purpose you can bear almost any "how" to achieve it.

What Was the Most Difficult Thing You Have Had to Deal With?

This question leads you directly to your purpose. The answer varies for different people. To give you some examples, a person might say that it was when their child was diagnosed with autism. Some might say it was when their spouse left them. For others, it could be related to something they dealt with in their childhood. In my own case, the answer to this question is my parents' unhappiness and them not accepting me for who I am.

Because of this difficulty you encountered there probably is a cause you care deeply about. In general, we want to remove or correct a certain pain or suffering. Because we ourselves have suffered and found a way to the light, we want to help others find their way with more ease. When you really connect with what has been the hardest thing you have had to deal with in your life, you will understand your motivation and drive to do your work.

I have spoken openly about my unhappy childhood with my parents. They fought and yelled at each other often. I witnessed this pain and suffering in them and I also suffered as a result of not feeling accepted. Because of this suffering, I have a strong desire to free people from the past. This is how I came to choose coaching as my life's work. Through this motivation I was able to focus on my business, despite the fact that I started from scratch with no money available to invest. Taking my business off the ground was difficult, but I had a strong drive to make it work.

Now it's your turn to answer the question: what was the most difficult thing you've had to deal with in your life? See what you can do to help others overcome similar difficulties. This is the most valuable lesson you can share with the world because you are drawing on your own experience.

Your work is more powerful and unique this way and it results in success and abundance. People with a problem similar to the one you had are seeking you out specifically because they know you will understand them, you will be compassionate, and they will trust you to guide them because you have figured it out yourself.

What is Something Your Younger Self Would Have Needed to Have or to Know?

The answer to this question can be as simple as someone to believe in me and support me. Or it could be a particular service or a certain product. What is something that your younger self could have used to move forward with more ease?

We follow our purpose in a desire to serve the world, but this undertaking is enhanced when it also serves us to grow, to heal, and to give ourselves some relief. We have to overcome the stigma of being called selfish when we take care of ourselves, and let go of the idea that being selfless and serving is noble. Our true purpose is balanced and serves both us and the world.

If your purpose does not include you, it might not be your spiritual path; it might just be a fabrication of your ego.

When you give some relief to that younger self, sometimes represented by your inner child, you are balancing giving with receiving. Your younger self might have needed guidance, and now that you are wiser you can guide others. I believe that through this process you heal that younger self.

In my case, while growing up no one believed in me. I was put down constantly and told I was not good enough and that I would never amount to much. I was called lazy, selfish, unintelligent, and bad. I was none of these. I believed in myself despite what they were saying. With the abuse I suffered I find it a miracle that I kept going and succeeding.

In my work now, I take great joy in being that person who believes in and instills confidence in others. I love looking into someone's eyes and saying to them, "Yes, I believe you can do it" and "I believe this is what you're meant to do". It really gives me unbounded joy when I see that shy look on someone's face. I can see by their expression that they are in disbelief: "really, you think I can do this?" I love giving that reassurance. I am getting emotional just thinking of this. I feel that by doing this for others, in some way, I am also giving this same reassurance to my younger self.

To align more with your purpose, a very good question to ask yourself is "what is something your younger self would have needed to have or know?" Then give these things to other people knowing that you are also giving them to yourself.

What Is Your Life About Now?

When you want to refine your purpose you need to see what your life is about right now and what you need right now. For example, if you are raising children, how is your business aligning with the fact that you have to spend time with your children. I know an entrepreneur whose son had terrible skin rashes and she developed a line of natural cosmetics to help him. Afterwards she sold the products at the local natural health store.

Other examples of what your life can be about might be the following: Have you just retired? Have you started college or other education? Are you solving a health issue? Are you consolidating a debt situation? Are you grieving? Are you looking for your soul mate? Have you just gotten married?

I believe that in order for our business to be sustainable, it has to encompass what is going on in our life at the time. If we keep this separate and apart from the other, life will be stressful and we will feel conflicted about where to dedicate our time.

What Do You Love Doing?

What is so easy for you to do? What is something that you enjoy so much that it does not even feel like work? What activity are you so passionate about that time flies by without you noticing when you engage in it? What gets you energized rather than feeling tired?

> *If your work leaves you more tired than energized, it might not be your purpose*

Some clients who are new to business ask me, "can I really set up my business and do something I really, really love?" The answer is a resounding YES! That is precisely how you want to set up your business because if you want your business to thrive it needs to be something you really, really love.

"You can only become truly accomplished at something you love. Don't make money your goal. Instead pursue the things you love doing and then do them so well that people can't take their eyes off you." Maya Angelou

Do you love being with people, analyzing data, talking, arranging flowers, or painting? You can make a business out of what might have started as a hobby because when you are passionate about something you do it well.

I love hosting and facilitating events because when I do them I feel like I am planning my own birthday party! I always loved my birthday parties even when it was hard for me to convince my parents to throw them. Gathering people and bringing them into an experience that will facilitate growth and connection is a true joy for me.

How to Find Your Own Purpose in Life

To exemplify the process of finding one's purpose, I'm including an edited transcript of an interaction with a live caller on the Entrepreneur Enlightenment radio show. I had not met this person prior to the call. Follow through and see how the questions discussed can lead to finding your purpose:

Irina: We have a caller with a question. Emma from Edmonton, are you on the line?

Emma: Thank you so much for taking my call, Irina. I'm really enjoying your show.

Irina: Thank you. Please share a bit about your business so that we have some background. Where are you now and how do you relate it with your purpose?

Emma: I am working every day on my spiritual path and on my journey, but lately I am really feeling a strong desire to start my own type of spiritual business. I have some blocks and I am not really sure what direction I want to take. I was wondering what your advice might be and if you could suggest where to start.

Irina: Let's go through the questions I mentioned. When answering you do not have to give personal details about yourself if you don't want. Let's start. What has been the most difficult thing for you in your life?

Emma: Um, probably some self-confidence. Doubting myself and not knowing what I could do or if I would be good enough to do it. I have ideas about what I want to do but I never push through with what I feel strongly about doing.

Irina: Since you said that doubting yourself has been the most difficult thing in your life, let's see how you can help others to not doubt themselves. Tell me a little bit about your skills, your talents, and your experiences. What makes you unique? Also, what spiritual modality have you learned?

Emma: I have learned Reiki and I have also taken a dousing course. I feel that my intuition is coming in stronger lately when I listen to it. I have also worked for many years with children so I feel that I have special talents working with children. I feel I understand them and relate to their feelings. I don't know if I would incorporate children in my business but I do have a strong calling to be working with children.

Irina: If you feel this strong calling then definitely children will be involved in your business. You will have to wait and see as there are many ways to work with children. Some people work directly with children and some people work with children indirectly through their parents. If you have a strong calling, always follow it. You said the most difficult thing for you to overcome was doubting yourself. You also indicated that you are trained in Reiki, dowsing, and intuition. I am picking up on what you are saying which is very interesting because dousing is something one does to be more certain of something. Is that right? Like when you are uncertain you douse and you find the answer.

Emma: That's right, yes.

Irina: It is as if you doubt yourself less because you are dousing to find the answer. Do you see how they are related? Doubting yourself with dousing and intuition. Also we know that when you do Reiki, blocks are removed, the body heals, and the energy aura is healed. What are you doing in your current career or what did you do previously?

Before the birth of the Entrepreneur Enlightenment Academy, I was a professional engineer. You might ask: what does engineering have to do with spirituality and business? Well, my analytical brain, and the way I solve problems in a logical manner, helps me in connecting the dots quickly from what people say to me and what comes to me in an intuitive manner. In other words, whatever you have done before will help you in your future business. So what is something that you have done? What was your training previously?

Emma: Well, I did take my Early Childhood Education and I worked with children for many years. I had my own daycare as well and I also was a property manager for a few years because I really enjoyed working with groups of people. These are the things that I have done in the past.

Irina: Do you see how they start to come together? You worked with children and owned a daycare, which means you managed a group of children and a group of parents. You were also a property manager. These are all really useful skills which will help you to move into your purpose-driven business. This is what will make you unique. You have the skills required to work with children. You also said that you were thinking about opening your own business and that you have some blocks. Tell me about some of your concerns or doubts.

Emma: I guess the biggest would be concerns about how to become successful or independent with running my own business compared to working for someone else. That is probably my biggest concern; that I will not be able to keep busy with it and get the word out there. These are probably my biggest blocks.

Irina: This is interesting because you said that what was hard for you to deal with was doubting yourself. Now when you are starting your business you are doubting yourself. Despite this you still have to take action. To me it feels as if your path to confidence is through this business. This is how you will grow more and how you will become independent. Is there a time in your life or in your early childhood when you were not allowed to be independent or when you felt a strong drive to be independent?

Emma: Yes, I could see that. I could see that there was some of this that was keeping me back from my independence. I can feel that was the case definitely in my younger years.

Irina: This is what will happen if you run your business: you will grow. I don't know your financial situation or if you have people depending on you or not, but you can always find a way to transition from where you are into your new business. It takes time to put yourself out there, to put your name out there, and to do all the things that you want to do. I definitely see that this path will give you independence and it will give you more confidence in yourself. You will also be helping children develop confidence.

Emma: Yes, exactly. This makes a lot of sense.

Irina: Do you feel that you can move forward now?

Emma: Yes, absolutely. I feel it has all come together. You really helped me to understand that if I can go out in confidence then I can help children to become confident and independent. It is really important to create these traits with children while they are at a very young age. I feel that I would be good at doing this especially after I have gone through all of this myself, pushing through this myself and gaining my own independence.

Irina: Exactly! If you need more support, reach out to me. Thank you so much for the question and for providing this opportunity for the listeners to work through this with you.

Have you enjoyed my conversation with Emma? It is a perfect example of how to find your purpose in life and how to do your work. As I have seen with my clients, establishing your business is indeed a way to grow yourself. It's a way to challenge yourself more, to move forward in your life, and to do the work that you are here on earth to do.

Align Your Business with Your Purpose

Many people search for their purpose. We want to know we matter, that our work matters; we want to know that we have a purpose for being here on earth and that our purpose is important. We also have a desire to be good, to do good, and to follow our purpose.

The definition of enlightenment for entrepreneurs says that to be in a state of enlightenment you need to know that you have come into this life with an important purpose. Knowing that your purpose is important will help you move forward, giving you the desire to do better, to grow, to put your service or product into the world, and to make an impact.

Believing that you have a purpose and deciding to follow your purpose no matter what is a choice, and only you can make this choice.

Once you've made this choice you will need determination to stick with it even when you cannot see the way. The more you work on your purpose, the more the magic of life is revealed to you. Clients who came into your life are usually connected with your purpose.

Following my purpose helps me find meaning even in difficult situations. I teach what I experience; I teach what I learn. When I go through tough times I want to learn how to deal with the difficulties so that I can then teach the solution. This way I make progress even on the days when the sun is not shining. Knowing that I have an important purpose is what keeps me going, moving forward, and growing.

Everyone's purpose is important. There is not one purpose which is less or more important than another. When we do our work, we grow into the person we are meant to be: the person who can fill all of the space we came here to fill. Growing into the person we are meant to be is important in itself no matter what the outcome of our purpose is. Our purposes are all intertwined; therefore, we serve each other by doing our work.

Your Purpose Evolves As You Are Journeying Towards It

Your purpose is like the horizon. You are always following your purpose; you are always on your path. When things work well, know that you are going in the right direction. When things are becoming difficult, ask yourself if it is time to change direction. Don't stay in the same place too long wishing for things to be as they were. Know when to move on.

The purpose I started with when I left the corporate world and opened my own business is not the same purpose I am working with now–it's a continuation. Our purpose grows and opens up in front of us as we progress on the path and we need to fine-tune our direction as we go along.

When things became difficult in my corporate career, I realized that it was time to move on. My purpose was calling me someplace else. I started my coaching practice with the desire to eliminate suffering and to show people another perspective on life.

Besides the suffering that I have personally seen and endured, I was also abused as a child. I was told that I was not good enough. I was constantly criticized, put to work, and not allowed to play. I felt a deep need for freedom. I wanted to be me and do what *I* wanted.

I constantly dreamed about running away from home. When I graduated from university, I accepted a job far away from where my parents lived. Later, I came to Canada thinking that if I went really, really far, I would be free and no longer be bothered by their opinions of me. Here in Canada, I built a good life for myself. I thought that my childhood pain was all forgotten and that I was free. This was all shattered one day when an unpleasant event at work brought back the feeling that I was all too familiar with: I am not good enough and I am not accepted for who I am.

Through this I understood that as long as we do not free ourselves in our mind, we are not completely free despite the ability to do as we wish and go where we please. We have to free ourselves from second-guessing ourselves and the negative self-talk, and we need to release the subconscious programming.

As I worked on this, freedom from the past became more and more important to my work and to my purpose. My clients benefited in the process and freed themselves from their own troubles.

Through my coaching I encountered entrepreneurs who were struggling in their own business and were afraid to lose this freedom and have to go back to work for someone else. I saw how powerless they felt. At the time I was already gaining good traction in my business. I decided that I wanted to do something about this and help people establish their own thriving businesses. I believe everyone has the right to be free, to follow their purpose, and to find fulfillment and happiness.

My purpose initially evolved from my strong desire to eliminate suffering to helping free people from their past programming. It then shifted slightly to focus mainly on entrepreneurs. Although I knew business fundamentals from my corporate career, I had to first learn the ins and outs of having my own business before I could work with entrepreneurs. Only then was I ready and able to teach others how to follow their own purpose, how to stay on their path, and how to make money in their business.

What I do now encompasses all that I did before. It grew to helping entrepreneurs while combining my three main talents: business, spirituality, and personal development. I love teaching entrepreneurs how to make at least corporate-level income while they stay true to their purpose so they can be free and fulfilled.

Could my purpose shift again? For sure! My grand vision is to contribute to the world's peace. When people make good money from their purpose-driven business, they have the incentive to stay committed despite the inherent difficulties that come with entrepreneurship. When people feel free to do what they love, they are happy. With freedom comes inner peace. World peace is possible when the majority of people have inner peace.

I hope my example gives you some food for thought and motivates you to start somewhere knowing that your purpose might evolve in time.

When You're Unsure About Your Purpose

You figured out your purpose and you were doing fairly well following your path, but then something happened that left you in the dark. Or maybe you were never quite sure of your purpose and you think you have not yet started your journey. What do you do now?

Some people stay stuck because they say they do not know what their purpose is, or they say it is not clear what to do next. I believe that this is a self-sabotaging technique fabricated by the ego to keep you safe, to keep you in your comfort zone.

Being around thousands of entrepreneurs from all over the world, I have seen that everyone has an idea of what their purpose is, even if it is vague. What keeps people stuck is the fear of criticism and fear of the unknown. As a result, they don't take much action. I often hear people say that they would love to set up their own business but they do not know what their purpose is.

Deep down we all know our purpose, but the voice might be too small and the fear too big; the confidence too small and the doubt too big. In this case it feels easier to say that you don't know what your purpose is. If that is what you feel, do something–anything. Take action. Start where you are and do something, whatever that is. You cannot find where a road leads if you don't start traveling.

I would like to reassure you that you are on the right path even if sometimes you are not sure. There is not only one road leading to your purpose. There are many. As long as you are moving forward, you are generally okay.

By doing something, you have the chance to observe and adjust what you are doing and change course if necessary. You will never be completely sure before you start. The assurance comes from doing and observing what works and what doesn't.

When we are fully aligned with our purpose, life is truly magical. My life is so magical; I never want to give up teaching because I love it so much. All the clients who have come into my life feel so aligned. What they bring to me as problems are appropriate for my skills and also what I am working on developing. This just keeps me going further and further.

Following your purpose is a journey and I have seen many times that it is not a simple journey. It takes immutable commitment and comes with a lot of frustration. It requires a big investment of time, energy, and trust.

It is a great feeling to have a business that aligns with your purpose. When you see the return on your investment in both fulfillment and money, it is a great confirmation that you are doing your life's work. All those who called you a dreamer or thought you lost your mind, all those who told you to get a "real" job can now be silenced.

Following your purpose is a real job especially when it pays you real money.

Why is it Hard to Get Support for My Purpose?

This is a question I often receive. My answer: first let go of the expectation that you need to be supported or approved by others in order for you to follow the path you feel called to follow. The basic premise is that your purpose is unique to you. Only you are called to do what you do in your particular way, no one else.

In order to follow your unique purpose, you have to give up on wanting other people to understand you. It is hard for others to understand what they do not feel. It is hard for others to be supportive if they maybe feel threatened by your ideas or your pursuit of your purpose. This is why when you commit yourself to your purpose you need to also learn to be empowered. By doing so, you are able to stay true to who you are despite external pressures.

The more you crave the support of others and their approval, the more resistance you will encounter. When you try to convince others or gain their approval, you waste precious energy that can instead be put towards the advancement of your purpose. Only you know what you need to progress with; only you see the vision of your purpose.

Don't I Need the Approval and Support of My Family?

Answer: We have to communicate with those who share their life with us and with those who are affected by our decisions, but we do not need them to say, "Bravo, I understand what you want, and I support you 100%".

When we want approval, we in fact might want to remove responsibility from ourselves and give it to that person. We want to be assured that if we fail we have someone to share the responsibility with. "You thought this was right too." This is what you would say to your partner or spouse if they felt that you wasted money and time investing in your business.

The big questions for you are:

➤ Do you fully support yourself in your endeavor?
➤ Do you believe in yourself enough to give your purpose all you've got?

If you do, then others will have no choice but to either believe too or at least give you their vote of confidence for you to give it a go.

Wouldn't it be awkward at the end of your life to meet your Creator who asks: have you fulfilled your purpose? And for you to answer, "I would have but my husband did not agree." This would be embarrassing, right? This is not a valid excuse. If you fully support yourself, you will find a way to get the support you need from your family or you will create a way to go without it.

Entrepreneurship is a difficult game that requires mental toughness, confidence in yourself, and a lot of commitment, stamina, courage, and determination. You must give your purpose a go–better still give it all you've got.

The reason why it is difficult to get support for your purpose is well illustrated by my favorite quote of all time:

> *"Those who were seen dancing were thought to be insane by those who could not hear the music." Friedrich Nietzsche*

This is why others cannot support your dancing or dance with you; they don't hear the music. Either you sing the music to them by sharing your vision, by staying open and explaining what you want, why you want it, and how is it going to work–or you get used to being fine dancing by yourself. The only thing you cannot do and that you should not do is settle for average because others do not understand. YOU CANNOT STOP DANCING my friend. You must dance no matter what. Dance to the sound of the music of your soul.

If you are lucky you can dance with your partner and you can have your music synchronized to their music. If you chose right, dancing together is more fun. You can dance with your entire family, your children and parents too. Make your own luck by negotiating, explaining your tempo, and understanding what the other person hears in terms of their music. This is how you get to thrive.

CHAPTER 3

Find Your Niche to Thrive in Business

I hope you now have more clarity on your purpose. I believe our ultimate purpose in life is love: to love who we are, to love the people we come in contact with, and to put love into the world through our work. Finding your niche is closely tied to what you love, and this is what we will explore next.

This chapter will help you define your niche by exploring who you connect with best, what segment of the population you love the most, and what brings you the most joy. Once you have defined your niche, we will discuss what to do when people outside your niche are interested in your services.

Through my experience in working with entrepreneurs, I have come to see that it is easier to grow your business when you have a defined niche. I believe that your niche is closely related to your purpose.

The Definition of Niche

In the dictionary, niche is defined as "a comfortable or suitable position in life or employment." An example is, "He is now a partner at a leading law firm and feels he has found his niche". A synonym for niche is an "Ideal position". You may hear someone saying, "She found her niche in life".

In the business sense, niche represents a "specialized segment of the market for a particular kind of product or service". Also, niche is "denoting or relating to products, services, or interests that appeal to a small, specialized section of the population".

The Paradox of Niche

Most entrepreneurs have difficulty with the word "small" in the definition above. When setting up your business, you are hungry for clients. The idea of restricting your offer to a small segment of the population is really scary. It's counterintuitive, right? At the beginning when you have no clients you feel that you need to tell as many people as you can about what you offer. Hearing that you have to restrict your offer to a small segment of the population might scare you.

Here is the paradox: when you restrict your offer to a specific segment of the population, within a specific area of expertise, you in fact increase your chances of getting clients. When you clearly define who you work with, potential clients easily recognize themselves in your message and connect with you. This is also when you get more referrals because friends, family, and previous clients understand who you serve. While it may be a paradox, defining your niche is powerful.

Finding your niche is an important step when building your thriving business. When you try to sell to everyone, your message is so general that your potential clients cannot identify with it. As a result, they cannot make the decision to buy.

Whenever you get scared that your niche might be too small, remember that there are 7 billion people in this world! No matter how small you think your niche might be, you still have lots of potential customers.

Narrowing your niche helps your business thrive because more potential clients can identify with what you do. They will be able to connect with you more deeply and make the decision to buy.

Let's take a look at an example. In Chapter 2 we read the transcript from a conversation with a live caller where she was talking about wanting to become a Reiki practitioner. If she tells someone that she's a Reiki practitioner, that person may not know if they need Reiki, or even what Reiki is all about. Because the potential client is not sure what she's offering, they may avoid connecting with her any further.

Let's change this scenario to a defined niche. Imagine that now this entrepreneur says, "Hi, I do Reiki for kids who doubt themselves, and I help them gain their independence". This is a completely different story, right? Now it gets interesting! After hearing that, I may think of my nephew because I believe he doubts himself, and bingo: we've got a connection! I may then refer her services to my nephew's mother.

This is the power of defining who you are working with—your niche—and specifying what you do for them. In the next chapter we'll talk about how to present your services so you're emphasizing your results rather than your methods, like Reiki, which will help to clarify your message even further.

Narrow Your Niche to Gain Credibility and Clients

To clarify your purpose you need to define who you are and write down your skills, talents, and experience. This is very important as it allows you to discover your expertise. When you match your niche with this expertise you gain instant credibility and your chances to attract clients increase.

I'd like to share an example from a client who listened to the radio show just before having a private session with me. That day, I talked about purpose on the show, and she said she gained some insight about what her purpose was through listening. Afterwards, in her private session we took it further and discussed her niche stemming from her purpose. Later, when I received her notes from our session, I saw that she had taken the niche we discussed and had broadened it.

This client had extensive work experience in arbitration. In her private life she experienced a very long and painful divorce where she lost custody of her kids and then regained it. We defined her niche as providing services for mothers going through divorce. This aligned with both her work experience and her personal experience. However, in her notes she broadened her niche to "working with people in crisis". This is vague. What kind of crisis: health crisis, relationship crisis, financial crisis? When you broaden your niche too much, your potential clients glaze over your marketing material because they don't connect with it. Even your supporters, friends, and family who would like to help you get more business would not able to understand exactly what you provide.

If my client specifically said she works with mothers going through a divorce and helps them with this relationship crisis, it would be easier for her potential clients to recognize themselves in that message.

In addition to making it easy for the right people to connect, having a niche informs the people who don't need your service. The sooner someone recognizes they are not your client, the better it is for them and for you as it conserves precious time. Good marketing attracts the people who need your service or product and repels the ones who don't.

Many new entrepreneurs have this tendency to broaden their niche; I've done it myself at the beginning of my career. Having a broad niche might lead to less clients, not more clients.

I know that creating a narrow niche might scare you, but this is what will help you to define your market. Especially at the beginning of your entrepreneurship journey, it is important to start with a narrow niche. As your business grows, you can go broader if you feel the need. Take a deep breath and feel comfortable knowing that defining your niche is a way to success.

Having the Right Niche is Purposeful and Loving

Your niche stems from your purpose; your niche is aligned with your spiritual path. There needs to be a higher purpose for everything we do. When we work in our niche, we are opening ourselves up to the people who might have a soul contract to work with us.

When you have a defined niche, it's easier to make money and thrive! When you specialize, you become more and more versed in what you do because you address specific problems on a regular basis, rather than a broad range of problems once in a while. Your business is more sustainable because as you address the same problems over and over, you require less preparation time.

When I started coaching as a Strategic Intervention coach certified by Tony Robbins, I didn't specialize in anything. At the time I had an office on the main street of a city and the sign on the building said Life Coaching. Anyone in that area was welcome to come in and request my services. In the same day I had people wanting to lose weight, wanting to improve their relationship with their spouse, wanting to organize their house and get rid of stuff. I also had business clients.

I quickly realized that this is not the best way for me to want to help all people with all of their problems. There were a few cases where I had little expertise in the area and I was dissatisfied. Personally, I wanted to be an expert. This is why I chose entrepreneurs as my niche. The more I coach, the more I know. Plus, I have my own journey and expertise to draw on.

There is power in staying in your specialty. You need to feel good about your work because in business you need confidence in order to succeed. If you feel that you didn't help, then your confidence in your abilities goes down. And when your confidence goes down, you don't put yourself out there as much. When you are losing your confidence you are losing your ability to make money. This is why it is not good to go in too many directions at once.

When you stay with one direction you stay focused on what you know, and through practice you get more experience. When people get results by working with you, they will send you referrals and you will be able to charge higher rates for your services.

When I work in the areas I have expertise with–for example, becoming truly free of past conditioning–I can confidently stand there and say: I know it hurts, I know it's painful, but I know it will pass once we quiet the critical voice in your head. I have that conviction because I've been there–I've done it! I know it's not easy, but I know it's possible. I know that at the end of the process, my client will feel so free it will be hard for them to believe that they were once so constrained.

Remember to bring what you have actually experienced into your work. Define who you're working with and what you are specializing in. This is how to establish your niche and harness the power of your experience. As a result, your confidence will grow and your clients will be happy and rave about you. They will thank you for how much you have done for them. More importantly, you will know that you have made a difference in your clients' lives. You will be able to celebrate your clients for achieving great results and to be proud of your work.

Here are some questions that will help you define your niche:

1. What is your expertise?

In a corporate career you get raises or promotions as you gain more experience in your field; similarly, in your business you can gain credibility and charge more if you have the experience to back up what you do. Having your niche in an area where you have expertise and experience makes it easy for your clients to trust you and connect with you.

The area where you have the most experience is also likely the area you are most comfortable working in. As you grow your business and gain more familiarity in other areas, you can expand your niche. In the beginning, however, it's good to stay in the area where you have the most knowledge.

2. Who do you care about the most?

Who do you care about the most: kids, young adults, women, men, or the elderly? For example, some people care about seniors and helping them with that stage of their lives. What segment of the population do you care about the most? This includes age group, but can also include industry, like nurses, managers, entrepreneurs. Decide who you care about most.

In the example from Chapter 2, Emma cared more about kids and felt her purpose was to work with kids; therefore, her niche would be kids.

3. Where would you like to make a difference?

Where would you like to make a difference: in your city, province, country, or internationally? It is important to know where you will focus your business.

I used to focus my in-person events for local entrepreneurs because I loved bringing them together to network, mastermind, and create unforgettable in-person experiences. Although I still teach locally, I've now expanded the events and the Academy to a global audience through the use of technology.

I have clients who like to travel; they like to take people on retreats to Costa Rica or Bali. Knowing yourself well will help you decide where you would like to make a difference. It can be anywhere in the world!

4. Who do you connect with most easily?

When you walk into a group of strangers with all sorts of ages and backgrounds, who do you feel you connect with the most? In my case, I connect well with entrepreneurs because they are determined to create something. They have goals; they are determined to grow and they place an importance on personal development. For me, entrepreneurs have interesting things to say, they don't just focus on small talk. Instead, they talk about their goals; they ask meaningful questions. This is why when I am in a group of people I don't know very well, I tend to connect with other people who are also in business. I like to talk with them about what they do, how it is going, what works, and what doesn't.

This is an important point to consider because if you want to serve people whom you cannot easily connect with, building a successful business will be hard. But if you are able to walk into a group and you instantly connect with a certain type of person, this is a good indication for your niche. The caller in Chapter 2 said she was drawn to helping kids. I would be curious to find out what would happen if she went to a wedding where she didn't know many people: would she end up playing games with the kids? That would truly confirm that she really connects with kids if that's where her heart goes.

Some people connect with their ethnic or cultural group. At one point I thought I could work with people who are new to the country because I came to Canada with only two thousand dollars, two suitcases, and a promise of a job, not having anyone here to support me. I know the struggles newcomers face, and since I found my way I thought that maybe I could help other people integrate into Canadian society. I later realized that this wasn't my purpose, so I moved on.

Don't expect to come up with your niche today. Be easy on yourself if you cannot figure it out right away. This is a complex process. In the next few weeks observe who you connect with most easily.

5. What are you most passionate about?

When you do what you're passionate about and you do it with people you connect with easily, your work is joyful.

> *If you do what you love to do for the people you love to connect with, in an area where you have the most expertise, your work will be easy and you will thrive.*

When you try to find your specialty, look at what you love to do. Do you love helping people? Do you love analyzing data and being behind the scenes? Maybe you love talking with people in person? In the end, we all help people through our work. All of our activities help people because that's the purpose of a business: to serve and to fulfill a need. Think about what you like. Do you like to be creative? Do you like painting? Arranging flowers? How can you specialize in that area for the segment of the population you want to work with?

Sometimes our hobby can become our business. Personal development was my hobby. I used to work in nuclear engineering, which is a completely different field than coaching. Because of my difficult childhood, I developed an interest in personal development. I wanted to understand how the mind works and why we suffer. I wanted to know what I could do to alleviate that suffering. As a teenager, I read psychology magazines. My entire life has been focused around personal development: I read self help books, I continuously took self-help courses, and I even got a coaching certification before I knew that I would ever want to practice coaching as a profession.

If you have a hobby, then think about how you can turn that hobby into a business. When you're passionate about something, you will do it well; and when you do something well, clients (and money) will come to you! This is the joy of doing business aligned with your purpose, and this is how you thrive both in business and in your personal life.

When People Outside Your Niche are Interested in Your Services

When you define your niche, you have better chances of thriving in business. You are in a better position to grow your business and to be where you want to be because it is easier for you to attract clients. In addition, you get better results because you have expertise in that area and that helps your confidence grow.

When you work in your niche, you are actually serving your purpose. You're serving the people with whom you may have a soul contract to work with.

But what do you do when people outside your niche are interested in your services? You have to decide if it feels right for you to serve them or not.

If it doesn't feel aligned, if it doesn't feel that you have the experience, it is better to refer them to someone else. It's helpful to keep a roster of colleagues who specialize in other areas that are complimentary to yours. This is courteous for the client as you still help them by redirecting them to a specialized practitioner, and it's also a nice way to build your network by supporting other practitioners, service providers, and businesses. Those other practitioners may do the same for you.

If it feels right for you to serve them and you have the expertise, do serve them. Look for cues to see if you are meant to work with this person. Maybe there is a higher purpose for taking them on as a client; maybe your purpose is shifting. You don't know the whole spiritual plan.

I work with entrepreneurs. Once in a while, I meet people who want to work with me but they are not entrepreneurs. They are not even thinking about opening a business, but they need to work on becoming truly free from their past and abusive relationships. This is one of my specialties and the title of my upcoming memoir, *Becoming Truly Free*. Because of my personal experience in this area, I'm passionate about freeing people, and I accept to work with the right ones even if they are not in my niche of entrepreneurs.

When those people want to work with me, I try to find a connection and see if we are really meant to be together. I remember at one exhibition I participated in, someone sat down at my booth. We exchanged just a few words, and then she started crying from the energy of the connection. She told me a bit about why she was crying: her mother lost her mom when she was five years old. And guess what, my mother lost her mom when she was five years old too. From this short conversation I knew immediately that we had a purpose together. She wished for a business, but she was not close to opening one yet. The logical part of me kicked in and asked if I could really help this person get a return on her investment. This person didn't even have a business. I felt spiritually connected to her so I said yes. Bless her heart, we did extraordinary work together: it was deeply healing for her, and it also touched me.

I shared this story so you don't turn people away just because they are not in your niche. If you feel a connection, then work with them. Defining your niche helps you to focus your marketing efforts, be clear who you're serving, and pinpoint your purpose. The majority of people you serve will be in your niche. However, if someone comes to you with a problem that you know you can solve, by all means serve them.

If I was strictly a business coach teaching only about marketing and sales, and this lady came to me with her emotional story about her mother, then of course our collaboration wouldn't have worked. But because I combine business with spirituality and personal transformation, I knew I could help her with what she was experiencing. I feel I have touched her life in a meaningful way, and while the return on her investment was not monetary, it was something much more meaningful: a life free from suffering.

I hope this story helps you feel more comfortable defining your niche. You don't have to only work with the people in your niche; you can work with people who you feel a connection with. However your marketing needs to be very clear and specific to your niche so you can attract clients with ease.

Dance with the Universe

When you are searching for the best way to do business, don't go at it alone, work with the Universe. This is like dancing with a partner. Dancing with someone is a complex experience: you listen to the music, you pay attention to where your partner is moving next, you lead, you move, and you follow. It's a give and take. Combine what you get through your logical thinking on which niche is best for you with the clues you get from the Universe. Pay close attention to the signs you receive.

When I started coaching, I worked with everyone who needed to achieve results. As I progressed, I realized that I needed to make some changes. I was at crossroads, deciding who to focus on. I asked the Universe for help.

Logically, I was thinking that my niche could be managers in a corporate environment because I had extensive managerial experience. By that time my business was stable and I was doing well. I spoke to the Universe: you know, I'm a bit confused here, please help me out. I made a wish. I set an intention. I told the Universe that the first person who calls me and becomes my client will indicate my niche. The rule I set was that they had to call me on their own initiative.

The person who called me first was an entrepreneur from a business group I was a part of. Following the signs I received from the Universe, I decided that entrepreneurs would be my niche. They were people I connected well with. I like entrepreneurs because they make an impact in the world and through them my impact is multiplied.

This niche was perfect for me because I had an extensive business background. I have a business-focused mind and I like to strategize with people. When I found this niche through that caller that the Universe sent me, I felt aligned. This is how the Entrepreneur Enlightenment Academy was born.

I want you to know that you will constantly refine your business. You can never say my niche is selected, my marketing is done, and my website is complete. You will keep refining your niche and your business as you grow.

CHAPTER 4

Lead with Client Results and Your Story

Once you have established your niche, you are ready to start writing your marketing copy. The strategy I will teach you here is to lead your marketing pitch with the results your clients obtain by working with you, instead of focusing on your methods or your process. Then we'll talk about why it is important for you to share your story. We'll also discuss the critical elements of a website that connects with the heart of your potential client. This is important as many website professionals offer you a nice-looking website, but if it doesn't connect with your niche, the website doesn't serve its purpose. A website is not about pretty pictures and clever words, it's a place where your potential client lands and connects with you, finds your vibration, and becomes inspired to dig further.

Determine the Results Your Clients Get

Remember the Reiki practitioner we discussed in the last few chapters? We focused her niche so that instead of just saying "I do Reiki" she now says "I do Reiki for kids who doubt themselves and I help them gain their independence." What is the result in her message? In this case, she helps kids gain their independence—this is what her potential clients would be interested in. That is the result of her work.

Your potential client is first interested in the results they will get, not in your method or the process you use to attain those results. Think about the marketing message for massage therapy: it talks about relaxation and about how your body will be more alive, more energetic, after the massage is over. It does not say that the therapist will stretch your muscles with their hands and sometimes push their elbows into a sore spot until you tear up. If that was the marketing message people probably wouldn't go for a massage! We go to massage therapy for the benefit of relaxation, to give our body vitality and stretch. To get those results, we have to put up with a bit of discomfort. Do you get the idea? For example, when you go to the orthodontist, you buy the straight teeth, not the braces. When you go for a facial, you buy the glowing skin, not the sticky mask that makes your nose itchy.

When you speak about the results you offer, think about what your clients want to achieve. Then find a way to explain the results without describing the modality. Some processes are not that well known, so instead of spending time educating your clients, it's better to share what the results will be and how they will benefit from them.

For example, your method could be performance coaching, Akashic record, astrological chart, Rainbow Energy Healing, spiritual director, nutritionist, or life coach. Share with potential clients what they will experience, and how this will help them get from where they are to where they want to be.

Take a moment and write down what results you have received for yourself from your method, and the results that you know your clients have experienced.

Your customer will ask you questions before they decide if they want to work with you. There may be questions like: What will I find out if you read my Akashic record or my astrological chart? What will

I experience if I come to Reiki or Rainbow Energy Healing? What is the result and how will this help me get to where I want to be?

There is a marketing concept that says that for effective marketing you need to be joining the conversation your client already has going on in their head. If you do that and your marketing provides the answer to their questions, describes how your service meets the need they have, then they will respond and engage with you.

While I was doing the radio show I was searching for social media assistance. The conversation I had in my head was something like: How does this work? Will this person take what I have and manage my social media accounts on their own? Will this save me time? If I saw a social media manager's marketing message saying they would save me time, I would definitely want to hear more from them. If they indicated that they would listen to my radio show and extract important pieces and write my blogs for me so I didn't have to do it myself, I would be sold! That would get me to pay attention.

The same goes for your customer. Find out the conversation in your potential client's head and then connect the results of your work with how you can help them. This is how they will want to know more. This is why they will engage with you and possible become your client.

Leading with your results instead of your methods is important especially when you have multiple tools in your toolbox. If you talk about your process, you end up restricting yourself. When your marketing focuses on results, then you can use whatever tools you feel guided to use to help your client achieve the results they are after. This makes your work much easier for you and makes it more valuable for your client.

In my case, I combine Strategic Intervention coaching, business coaching, angel guidance, and Rainbow Energy Healing. I use any of those methods to help my clients achieve results. Some sessions can be mostly business coaching, some energy healing. I cannot tell ahead of time.

The way you combine your modalities and your experience is what makes you unique. Often, while your business is growing, you might add new processes. You don't want to be bound to only one modality. You want to have the flexibility and the freedom to use whatever tool you have in your toolbox that is appropriate for the task at hand. This is another good reason to stay focused on the results.

There was once a potential client who wanted to work with me, but he only wanted the business strategy, not the intuitive guidance. He didn't want me to read angel cards for him. It was difficult for me to accept this condition. I have to be authentic to myself and complete my work in an effective way without restrictions. When I feel that drawing angel cards could help figure out the path forward much easier than talking for hours, I have to have the freedom to use that method. As a result, we chose not to work together.

Talk about the results in your marketing material. The results my clients get from working with me as part of the Entrepreneur Enlightenment Academy are increased clarity, confidence, and ease. They learn how to thrive in business while following their purpose.

How do I do speak about results? I created a self-assessment tool that measures the level of authenticity, empowerment, and connectedness of the potential client. Once they fill out the assessment form and get their results, we have a conversation. Let's say they got 4 out of 10 for authenticity; I know then that this person needs more clarity into who they are and how they operate. We have a way to know the results they need to achieve, and we also have a way to achieve those results as we go forward with the coaching process.

The second result I offer is increased confidence. I've seen this problem over and over: it is hard to make money in your business when you don't have confidence. To be more successful in business, you need to have more confidence in yourself and what you offer to your customers. The part of the curriculum that helps with confidence is how to be empowered, how to let go of the past, and how to become your one and only authority figure.

The third result my program offers is ease in growing your business. I don't believe in hard work! Of course I believe in focused work, in dedicated work, in intentional work, but I don't believe in hard work when it makes you say, "Ugh, I don't like it". I don't believe in hard work that takes the energy out of you and leaves you depleted. In order to work with joy, you need to feel the flow and you need to be connected with other people who can support you. You need to be connected with a higher source like the Universe, God, or whatever you believe it to be. You need to be connected with yourself and feel your alignment and state of joy.

So in my case, my programs provide clarity, confidence, and ease and that is achieved through raising my clients' level of authenticity, empowerment, and connectedness.

Your turn now, what are the results your services or products provide?

Your Story Helps You Connect with Your Niche

Sharing your story is an integral part of your marketing material because it helps your potential customers connect with you. People buy from someone they know something about, someone they can trust. Since the introduction of online marketing, some businesses have lost sight of the fact that to sell we need to actually be connecting with other human beings. This is true especially in services. Personally, I only go for services to people I really like and trust.

When we know someone's story, we understand where they are coming from and we connect with them—we click. It's very important to share your story so potential clients can understand why you do what you do and why they should trust you.

The story you need to share is the story you don't want to share.

It's the story you maybe only share with your best friends. It is the true story, not the "look at me; see how many courses I've taken and how great I am" story. It's the story of the difficulties you've had and how you overcame them. It's the hero's story, and it's a difficult one to tell.

The first time I publicly shared my story of being an abused child was not easy. Before that time, someone would have had to really gain my trust for me to open up and share my story with them. I had volunteered for a project—a theatre performance where a group of women shared their raw stories as a way of inspiring healing through sharing and connection. I had to do a lot of healing and summon my courage to come to the place where I stood on a theatre stage and shared unpleasant truths about my parents. It was not an easy task. The reward of this courage was that so many people came to me sharing their own stories, and many people still remember that performance today after so many years.

Telling my raw story not only helped me heal, but it also helped other people heal. Do not feel shy about sharing your story. When you share your story, you transcend your ego and you go deeper into the healing process. You release shame and guilt and you give other people an opportunity to connect with you.

The Elements of Your Story

Here are four elements that every great entrepreneurial story needs to have:

1. **Your life before:** Start with describing your life before you began your business. Some questions to prompt you are: What were you doing before you started on this path? What was your life like then? What was going on?

2. **Your awakening:** You were going along with your life and some things were not working or something happened. Then you had an awakening! Maybe it was an event, a hardship, an accident, an illness or an epiphany. What was the life-changing moment?

3. **Your understanding:** How did you get to your new level of understanding? Talk about what you did after your awakening. Did you change career directions? Did you start taking some courses? How did you end up where you are today?

4. **Your confidence and results:** Lastly, write about how your confidence changed with the results you got for yourself and with your clients. If you're not yet in business or you've just transitioned and are starting out fresh, you may not have clients yet to talk about their results. That's completely okay. You can start with the results you have for yourself, and as you start working with people you can ask for testimonials and identify their results.

I didn't know from the beginning what the results of my coaching would be. I knew I would help my clients achieve their goals but that was all I knew. As I started to work with more people and received their testimonials, I saw that a lot of people spoke about getting clarity, even after one session. I heard that comment over and over. When I put my marketing materials together, I pointed out that the result of working together is clarity because that is what my clients said they benefited from the most.

The same goes for you: first pay attention to what you achieved for yourself, and then pay attention to what your clients are saying you helped them achieve. Sometimes our idea of the results we provide may differ from the client's actual results. The client's report of what they think they got out of your services is more important.

Take special note of what the clients you enjoy working with most say. Those are the clients you connect with at a deeper level. They are your most aligned clients. It's wise to put a little more weight on what those clients say rather than what the clients who are resisting your work say. Be sure not to lose your confidence when you have one client who says they have not achieved their goals—focus on the 99 other clients who are happy with what you have done for them. Those are the clients you want more of.

And for the ones who are resisting, know that everyone is on their own path. Sometimes people sign up to work with you when they feel connected, but later their ego resists your methods. It's okay when this happens—there will be a time when they will transcend their ego too, but now is not the time.

For you to get your business going, you need to work with people who get the results they want to achieve. You need to understand that you cannot be everybody's healer, everybody's coach, or everybody's therapist. This concept is hard to understand, especially for people in service-oriented businesses or spiritual people who want to help everyone. It's just not sustainable.

To recap, here's how to write your story: start with what you were doing before, next talk about the awakening and how you gained a new level of understanding. You took this understanding to solve the problem for yourself and then you offer it to other people. From the results they get you gain confidence in your work and then you offer it to others who can benefit from your expertise.

When you write your story, follow a logical path. Don't assume people know anything about you. Lead people from where your story began all the way to where you are now, but be sure not to burden the reader with unnecessary information. This is not your full life's story. This is a story meant to connect people with you and your business. If your potential client feels aligned after reading your story, they will want to reach out and talk to you.

To start, just write the story as it comes to you. It doesn't matter if the story is too long or too short, just write it down to begin with. Have someone else read it and help you discard the information that isn't necessary or add the missing parts.

While working on this book, I helped one of my clients write her story. She was asked to provide a bio for a clinic she works at, and didn't want to provide a resume listing her work experience; she wanted a story that would connect with her potential customers.

This is how we built her story and it's an example to help you better understand how to do yours.

She is now a naturopathic doctor. Her story of how she got here is an interesting one. When she was a young girl, she used to be a professional gymnast. If you know anything about sports and performance, the competition is quite high, as is the desire to belong. She wanted to fit in with some of the more advanced girls. She wanted to be part of this popular group and asked to join. They gave her some rules and one of them was to do what they do. Those girls were bulimic. My client made a choice to become bulimic in order to be accepted by that group. This meant she ate and then she made herself throw up.

It's a bit sad, isn't it: a young woman making herself sick just to belong. It's not hard to figure out that she didn't tell this story to many people. After a while, the bulimia became so bad that her body would respond automatically. Even if she ate just a piece of toast, her body would throw it up right away. It became uncontrollable and she was understandably worried and scared. She wanted to heal herself so she went to see a naturopath. During that time some of her family members were ill, including her mother, and she saw the side effects of the chemicals in traditional medicine. She already had a conviction that if she ever got sick, she would want to treat herself in a natural way with herbs, homeopathy, and naturopathy. Working with her naturopath helped her control her bulimia.

Things were going well for her after that. Her career as a gymnast was progressing. However, one day she fell and broke her knee. The doctor told her that she would not be able to compete anymore. Imagine how hard that is to hear. She became depressed and went back to her naturopath who helped her heal once more, and also inspired her to study naturopathy.

This is a brief account of her story and how naturopathy helped her heal, and this is why she is now offering this service to others. Don't you feel empathic just listening to her story? Do you feel a connection? If you know anyone with similar problems, you may even want to reach out to them to let them know of this naturopath.

It is powerful to share the story you don't want to share. It can be uncomfortable to share it, but it's a way to heal yourself, and it is very effective for your marketing message too. The bulimia story is a pretty sad story and my client had some shame around it at first. I hope her story inspires you to write your own story now.

Creating a Website that Connects with Your Client

Your website is a way for people to get to know you before they talk to you. Your website is the place where you send potential clients who want to know more about your services and what you can do for them. This saves you time as you don't have to keep repeating yourself every time you speak with a new person. Your website also gives the person who lands there the opportunity to move on if they don't feel a connection with you.

If you're just starting out in business, don't pay thousands of dollars for a website. Instead, make a simple website that includes the points below, and then you can expand and improve it as your business grows. Many entrepreneurs start their business by investing thousands of dollars into a fancy website and flashy business cards, and then they get discouraged that they spent all that money with little return. To start a business, the first thing you need is a customer.

As you start to make an income, you can invest a portion of it to upgrade your website and marketing materials.

1. **Your story:** As you probably guessed, your story is one of the critical elements of your website.

2. **Your clients' results:** Your website needs to focus on the results you will provide for your potential clients. Remember, try to connect with the conversation your customer is already having in their head.

3. **Testimonials:** It is really, really important to have testimonials. Ask for testimonials with every occasion; it's your right to have feedback on your work.

If you run events, one of the best practices is to have a feedback form to give to the attendees at the end of the event where they can write their thoughts while they are in the moment. Specifically ask your attendees to write a couple of sentences in the form of a testimonial and what they took away from the workshop or retreat. I find those feedback forms to be extremely valuable to extract content for both the results page and the testimonials page on my website.

Another reason to not be shy asking for testimonials is to know they are not for you; they are for your potential clients to help them decide to invest in your service or product. Testimonials tell your potential clients what they can expect. Ask for testimonials knowing that they serve others.

Getting a testimonial is not an ego trip where someone says you are great and they love your work so much. I do recommend you read testimonials when you need to increase your confidence, but it is not the main purpose of a testimonial.

If the fear of criticism prevents you from asking, accept that you are not everyone's healer or coach. Criticism shouldn't crush you and make you hide from the world. Learn to withstand it. I remember in my corporate career I was regularly delivering a seminar on a particular topic, and as I got the feedback forms reviewing my delivery I focused on the one or two that were critical instead of the dozens that were positive. In time I learned to stay focused on the positive ones. It's what matters most anyway.

The main purpose of testimonials is to give confidence to people who have the desire to work with you. Sometimes people don't fully trust the marketing copy. However, when they see somebody like them—who has been struggling with the same thing they have—got great results by working with you, they feel more guided to connect with you. Your potential client is unsure if your services will work for them. When they read a testimonial about someone else's struggle and how working with you has turned their life around, they will know that there is hope for them too.

When you ask for testimonials, ask for them in a way that prompts your clients to think about the results they achieved. If you don't specify this, your clients might just say how great you are, and that doesn't really say enough. You need a specific statement that speaks to the results you have helped your clients with. Put those testimonials on your website and use them as often as you can. If you have social media, put them there as well.

When you are starting out, if you don't have clients right away you may need to do an exchange of services or offer free sessions in return for a testimonial.

4. **Pictures of you:** I believe in authenticity and I really feel pictures have a special vibration. This is why I highly

recommend using your own photos on your website instead of stock photography.

Take pictures when you are working with a client, at your events, at an exhibit or trade show, or when you are presenting something. Those are the best pictures. Using stock photography is just occupying space. When I look at someone's website, I don't want to see a pretty woman on a massage table with a flower by her ear. I want to see a real client on their massage table. That attracts me more; that interests me more; that makes me analyze the picture and really see it. Use your own photos even if they are not professionally done because they are better at connecting with your client than any stock photography.

CHAPTER 5

Taking the First Steps with Your Purpose-Driven Business

Why is focusing on your purpose so important on your journey to success?

My purpose is to be a teacher and share what I've learned. If someone offered me $10 million and told me I could no longer teach if I took the money, I wouldn't take a cent. I find that my life has meaning when I teach. When I go through difficult situations in my life, I am always thinking about what lessons will emerge from those experiences. My personal life is enhanced by being able to learn and teach.

Ask yourself if your life would lose meaning if you were no longer able to fulfill your purpose.

When we fulfill our purpose, we fulfill it to serve others but also to grow ourselves. Sometimes when I teach, I feel that the lessons are also reinforced for me. Every time I prepare to lead a retreat, for example, I experience the retreat content beforehand: Becoming Truly Free, Manifesting Abundance, or Reinventing Your Business. Although I have taught those three retreats many times before, every time I go through them I am experiencing a new shift and a deeper understanding.

Without being able to do my purpose, my life would lose its meaning.

In this chapter we will discuss how you can begin the journey of fulfilling your purpose through your business. We will explore how you can get those first few clients, what strategies you can use when it comes to giving your service away free of charge, and why patience and discipline will be your best friends as you take those first steps.

Getting Your First Client

You've determined your purpose; you've determined your niche: the people you like to work with and the types of problems you solve. You have written your story that helps connect you with your potential client, highlighting the reasons you do what you do and your expertise. You've determined the results your work provides. Now it's time to get your first client!

Some people spend years and thousands of dollars designing their website, their business cards, and their marketing message, thinking this is what it means to have a business. I want you to understand something: you don't have a business unless you have paying clients. Having a flashy website and a beautiful business card does not mean you are in business. You are in business when you have clients who are willing to give you money in exchange for your service or product. I hope this busts some of the mystery for you and motivates you to take the first steps and get those clients.

I received a question from a listener of the radio show that I think many new entrepreneurs will relate to: How do I start promoting my first offer if I don't have a large network base? What else can I do besides networking?

Thinking that you need a large network base to start your business is a limiting belief. I've seen dreams killed in the first year of business because of the thought that one can only be successful with a large network base.

In the beginning you cannot handle more than a few clients anyway. If I had the business I have now in my first year, it would have crushed me because I didn't have the systems needed in order to operate smoothly and satisfy my clients. If I had as many clients as I have now, I would not be able to set them up, give them their content, and manage everything they need to succeed with the Academy. I needed to start small. I like organic growth anyway.

If you gain too many clients too quickly, you might not be able to serve them and meet their requirements effectively and that can take you backwards. Be careful what you wish for. At first, I recommend looking for one or two clients. I believe most people have a network large enough to find at least a couple of clients. Think about your network and identify a few people who could refer someone to you and help you get started.

You might be wondering how you will be able to replace your corporate income with just a couple of clients. My purpose is to help you make a corporate-level income so you can stay true to your purpose. This is just the beginning: you cannot become advanced before you are a beginner. You need to learn to walk before you can run!

My first event on my own had just three people, and one of them I almost dragged into the event free of charge. Many famous people had humble beginnings. Sometimes we forget that because we want to get directly to the end result. Dr. Wayne W. Dyer, for example, sold his first book from the back of his truck. In his book *I Can See Clearly Now*, he shares that he bought 4,000 copies of his first book to make the publisher print more copies.

Another interesting story is that of Sonia Choquette, a well-known Hay House author, which she shares in *Pebbles In The Pond: Transforming the World One Person at a Time*, compiled by Christine Kloser. At the beginning of her career, she was on a book tour and was invited to speak at a bookstore. Although there were 40 chairs set up, only one was occupied...by a homeless man. She was disappointed at the turnout, but took a deep breath and said to herself: "I have to do what I am here to do." She spoke with passion to the homeless man who was mostly snoring in his chair. The story has a happy twist: that talk at the bookstore was the launch of her career with Hay House. How? The bookstore manager referred her years later. She was impressed that Sonia did not complain about the turnout or blame anyone for the low attendance. Sonia did what she was there to do.

When you think that no one is there, remember that the Universe is there listening. Do your work with love and leave the rest to the Universe!

Thousands of people come to see Sonia now. I remember this story when I am disappointed by low registration for a retreat or webinar. My goal is to reach tens of thousands of listeners or millions of readers. I'm a big dreamer; I have big goals. I have to keep reminding myself that it takes time to build something. I only need to focus on delivering useful information; the rest is up to you to share and talk about it with others.

Remember to start small and aim for more as you go. Build your business as you build a house. You first need the foundation before you put up the walls and ceiling.

Giving Your Services Away for Free

Many entrepreneurs wonder whether it's okay for them to give away something for free. In certain cases this is a good way for people to sample your services and maybe buy from you or recommend you to others. In other cases, the reason for the free service should not be sampling. In coaching, for example, it's not a good idea to give sessions for free for sampling purposes. So the answer varies from case to case.

If you give away sessions for free, you need to do it in a strategic way.

When you are a beginner in your trade it's good to offer free sessions as a way to build your confrdence. Let's say you're a new Reiki practitioner and you've practiced in your classes, but now you want to see if somebody who's never had Reiki can feel the difference of your healing. This is a good opportunity to offer free sessions. This can be a way for you to build up your own confidence or to gain more experience. It can help you get your first testimonial, too.

Here are a few things to keep in mind when deciding on your free offers:

Offer free sessions to people you don't know rather than friends and family.

A word of caution: generally it is not a good idea to start by testing your new skill out on friends and family. We put a lot of weight on what the people closest to us say because we want their love and approval. If they don't compliment your skills or business, it might crush your confidence. Having confidence in yourself is your biggest asset in business. If you have confidence you will go out and make business. If you don't have confidence you will hide and not be able to get clients.

It's difficult for people closest to you to change their image of you. For example, if you give a coaching session to an older sister she may not listen to you; she may not fully engage because she is used to giving you advice, not the other way around. Just because you have a coaching certificate doesn't make her want to listen to you. It's not because she's mean. It's because she views you a certain way and it's hard to change that just because you have a piece of paper saying you are a certified coach.

It's a much better approach to give free services to people who don't know you very well or are meeting you for the first time. You have more chances of building your confidence with this option.

Let's say you do angel card readings. When you do a reading for someone in your family, you already know a lot about them. For example, if in your reading you uncover that they have disagreements with their boss, they may think they had already mentioned that to you. This doesn't build up your confidence. If you do a reading for a stranger and uncover that they are concerned about their son, imagine how your confidence will grow when they say "how did you know?!"

It is better to refrain from offering your new skill to friends and family. If you want to offer free sessions, work with people who don't know you that well.

Give free sessions to people who match your niche.

You need to be strategic about your free services so they help you build your business. Those sessions are not free for everyone; you don't want people to just take them and not care about the results.

Offer free services to a few people that match your ideal client. You want to work with your ideal client so you can understand more about their problems, learn about their issues, and figure out how to work with them.

To build your marketing material, offer a free session in exchange for testimonials. Testimonials from your ideal clients are more meaningful because your potential client can relate.

Start charging after three free sessions.

I recommend giving away three free sessions to three different people and then start charging for your services. Sometimes practitioners keep giving free sessions because they are afraid to sell. They feel they don't deserve money because they are not good enough. We will talk about this later.

After you give three free sessions, start charging about half of what an experienced professional in your area charges. When you are new, it's normal to be less comfortable or confident. This is why starting by charging half price helps. You can call this your introductory price. After five sessions at half price you can increase the price by 20 percent. Those are just guidelines, do what feels best for you.

The main point here is for you to charge for your work and increase your prices once you feel comfortable.

Manage ongoing free services carefully.

Offering a free session to someone who expresses interest in working with you on a long-term basis is a common strategy. It's called an exploratory session, discovery session, or get-acquainted session. The purpose for this session is to see if you and your potential client are aligned and will work well together.

You can choose to offer those free sessions, or complimentary sessions as I like to call them, in order to see if the person will benefit from working with you. This makes sense when they will be committing to a big-ticket item. You would not give a free session to see if the person would book just one session with you; this doesn't make sense. In this case they can take a risk, book your services, and pay for a session.

You can also offer free sessions to an influencer if you want them to experience your work and possibly connect you with their network. Be sure to make it clear why you are offering the free session.

To make sure people are committed and interested in your services, give them some homework that they will need to submit before the free session. This will prevent people from using your services just because they are free. When they do the pre-session work, they invest energy and that confirms that they have a genuine interest in working with you.

The prep work is for them to answer some questions. When you design the questions, make sure they will help you learn important information about the potential client's needs. Ask them to read certain things on your website, such as your story and testimonials. This will save time in your session as you will not have to explain to them what you do and why you do it. It will also prepare the way for the sale.

Just remember, you offer free sessions not because you are afraid to charge, but as a way for you to earn more business.

Ask for Referrals

The straightforward way to get your first client is to talk with people you know. Inform them about your new business and ask them directly if they can recommend someone to you. To make it easier for them to refer people to you, say that you are looking for people to sample your work. Be very specific about who you want to work with; specify your niche.

For example, the people who benefit most from my work are entrepreneurs who have had a hard upbringing. I believe for someone to be successful in business, they need to first let go of the pain of the past and become truly free. After that, they can apply solid business principles to expand their business. My vision is for new entrepreneurs to quickly make corporate-level income so they can stay true to their purpose.

Be specific when you ask people in your network to refer you and help you get those first clients. It is best if you speak directly with your contacts and supporters, but when that is not possible, sending an e-mail also works to take this first step.

Not Everyone Is Your Client

As a new purpose-driven entrepreneur, you are enthusiastic to get clients; you are eager to help. I know–I was too! As a result, I made an embarrassing mistake I will share with you so you can avoid it.

The business a few doors from ours was a hairdresser salon. When we were just starting out, the owner of the salon visited and shared one of her goals with pride. I was eager for clients and I hoped for her support as she knew a lot of people in the area so I offered to coach her to achieve her goal. I'll never forget the expression on her face: she was shocked! She could not believe I thought she needed to be coached. I probed further because I did not understand her reaction. I thought that she wanted to achieve her goal. I am a coach and I could help her. I worked with leaders in the past, so I felt somewhat qualified. Why did she get so upset? She gave me an interesting perspective that had not crossed my mind. She said: "how would you feel if we met downtown and I stopped you in the middle of the street and said 'your hair is so messy, how about you let me give you a haircut?'"

When I thought about it from that perspective, it made sense! So, you see, making an assumption that someone needs your services can be rude. Even if your purpose is to help people not suffer, you cannot push your services on people. I understand your desire to help but we need to understand their perspective too. People are living their lives and they are in whatever state they are; they don't need you to come by and say "hey, I think you have a problem—let me help you!" You are definitely not helping by doing this. I hope you remember this example. I will never forget it. Whenever I am tempted to tell someone that I think I can help them before they actually express that they have a problem, I take a deep breath and remember that I cannot help them because they have not expressed that they need my help.

Not everyone is your client: remembering this will save you some embarrassment. Another example: Let's say you work with parents and help them understand their children better. When you see a parent with a misbehaving child, you may think that they could use your help. However, remember they have not expressed the need for help, so don't offer your services until they do.

Nobody is your potential client until they tell you they have a problem **and** *they want help solving it.*

The Need for Patience and Discipline

I don't know about you, but I am not a very patient person. I like everything fast. Once I have a vision and I make a decision, I want to go! I've learned through my years in business that you need to build your business with patience. I've learned this, of course, after having stomped my feet with impatience many times. One day, exhausted and demoralized, I understood something that helped me become more patient: I'm in my purpose-driven business; therefore, I am in it for the long run. I never want to completely retire from this business because it is my purpose.

> *You are in your purpose-driven business for the long run; have patience.*

You are in this business because it is your calling. If you get frustrated because you are not seeing immediate results, remember that you are in it for the long run.

At the beginning of my business journey, I advertised a webinar and I didn't get a lot of registrations. Having just a few people registered felt as if I had failed. In business we need to be mindful of our energy. Being upset changes the vibration of our energy. Impatience is not a positive state; it is a negative state and it's hard to attract clients when we are in a negative state of mind.

We can learn from farmers and nature. When you garden, you plant a seed in the spring and then it needs time to grow. You have to water it, allow for sunshine, and protect the plant from weeds. In the beginning you don't see any progress, and then slowly something starts to show. If you continue nurturing the plant, it will eventually blossom.

It is the same with our business; it is the same with kids. Starting a business is like having a baby: the baby needs time and nurturing to grow healthy. When a baby comes out of the womb, you don't expect the baby to run. The baby needs lots of nurturing in the beginning.

After a few months the baby becomes stronger and learns to keep their head straight and then learns to crawl.

You wouldn't be impatient with a baby; why would you be impatient with your business? The majority of people I work with are people who had a successful career before venturing into entrepreneurship. When they start their business, they want to be at the same level of success as in their corporate career.

I know this because when I left my corporate job, I was a senior executive. I was one of just fifteen people in my field in the whole world. I was "somebody". I had results and I was recognized for my work. When I started my business, all of a sudden, I was "nobody". I didn't know how to do things. Nobody knew who I was. I had to start from zero.

In my corporate job I had a staff of 35 people. In my business there was no one to help me with tasks I didn't know how to do. Everything took longer and my impatience grew even higher. To calm myself down, I had to remind myself that it took me 18 years to build my corporate career from junior engineer to senior manager. I had to remind myself that when I was a junior engineer I didn't know how to read a schematic. I had mentors who taught me, and I had to go to the copy machine all by myself.

If you had a high-level position in a previous career, remember that this business is new and that you are a beginner. Allow yourself time to learn, to develop content, and to experiment. Be patient with yourself and know that all will progress in divine time.

The truth is that we need time to succeed. A few years ago, it wouldn't be possible for me to receive offers to do a radio show. Why? They wouldn't have been able to find me; I didn't have enough content, blogs, videos, or interviews. Everything comes in good time as long as you are staying the course.

Stay true to your purpose, do the work, keep the faith, and move forward.

Sometimes it is hard to keep going steadily when you the face the ups and downs of entrepreneurship. I recommend you find a mastermind group to be part of. I founded the Entrepreneur Enlightenment Academy to give people a way to connect and support one another. When you belong to a group of entrepreneurs who are growing together, you see others going through the same ups and downs. You see how difficult it is to get those first few clients or to fill the seats on the first few events, and you realize this is all part of the process and there is nothing wrong with you. When you don't have this group and you are alone looking at how others succeed without knowing what goes on behind the scenes, you start to think that you are doing something wrong.

When I joined a business mastermind lead by a successful business woman, I noticed a big difference in my ability to take action and stay the course. Before that I had been trying to get my business off the ground for a year. How hard can it be to establish my own business, I thought after I left my corporate life. After all, I raised my department's business by 600 percent up to $7 million! It's not the same when you do it alone and when you sell intangible items like coaching. I'm glad I joined the mastermind soon enough because it's much easier and much more fun to build a business when you learn from someone who has done it before, and with a group of people going through the same challenges as you.

Knowing that building a business takes patience and determination is important. Social media ads mesmerize a lot of entrepreneurs these days with programs that promise to help them grow their business to six figures in six months by working a four-hour week. This sounds so cool, especially to impatient achievers like me but building a business takes time.

I meet many spiritual people through my work. Some of them believe in the law of attraction. They think that if they can imagine it, it will come to them. Building a business takes action, strategy, and knowledge. It is comparable to building a house. You can imagine the house, visualize it, and see where the windows and the doors are. But in order for it to come into physical form, you still need to put one brick on top of the other brick and build it.

I invite you to have the patience and the tenacity to build a business that has a very good foundation. For example, some new entrepreneurs think that by participating in a summit they will get lots of people on their e-mail list and then they will sell them their services. At first the plan seems to work because there is a flurry of events, but then they end up feeling overwhelmed and cannot capitalize on the opportunity. This is because the business does not have a strong foundation.

I wasted about a year trying to sell my course online, following the get-rich-fast model. It didn't work because I didn't have a strong foundation. I discovered that I needed to first build my business in person, face to face. I needed to build my content, establish my reputation, and collect testimonials. I needed to be clear about the problems I could solve.

Remember this when you become impatient: you are in your purpose-driven business for the long run. A solid foundation will sustain your business so you can grow higher and higher like an oak tree.

PART 2

THE OUTER WORKINGS OF A PURPOSE-DRIVEN BUSINESS

CHAPTER 6

Learning to Love Marketing

"Suffering just means that you are having a bad dream. Happiness means that you are having a good dream. Enlightenment means getting out of the dream all together." Jed McKenna

When we are enlightened, we are not in a dream; we understand the spiritual truth that there is no good and bad. Everything that happens to us happens for a reason. Life is here for us to learn and grow, and to put more love into the world.

In the previous chapters we covered the internal work you need to do to establish your purpose-driven business: we defined your uniqueness, your experience, and the services you are providing. You learned how to align your business with your purpose. You worked on telling the story that connects your potential client with your work. You defined what results clients can expect to get by working with you. In Part 2, we'll cover what is needed to take your business out into the world. We start by focusing on marketing.

I receive many variations on the questions below from entrepreneurs around the world. I always have the same answer:

Can I be who I am and be successful? Yes!
Am I enough? Yes!
Is who I am needed? Yes!

In the last chapter we talked about the importance of patience and discipline. When we work in our purpose-driven business we can chose to never fully retire. I'm not planning to retire because I believe I will be even wiser when I am 90 years old. I'll have even more stories to share and they will bring more value to my work. I'll probably work fewer hours than I do now, but I will still teach and coach people. When we are in our purpose, all ages have a different value to bring to the world. We can shift the way we do business but we don't need to fully retire. I find this motivating. Don't you?

I have known people who count the years or months until their retirement. I feel sad for those people. When I hear someone say "I have five more years until I retire," it sounds as if they are in jail. Time is so precious. You can stay in any job, whether it is a corporate role or your own business, for as long as you find enjoyment and purpose. Anything longer makes no sense.

> *"Time is more valuable than money. You can get more money but you can't get more time." Jim Rohn*

If you are in a situation where you are counting the months or years, waiting for the time to pass, I invite you to discover more about your purpose. I invite you to learn more about who you are and how you can serve the world in your unique way. When you do what you love, time passes by quickly because you enjoy what you do and you feel fulfilled. Your life has meaning. I'm happy you picked up this book.

My mission is to support as many people to find their purpose and to become truly free to express who they are. My purpose is to teach you how to be both practical and spiritual and thrive as a result. I hope you join me in this movement and you do your part. Find your bliss, your happiness, and your freedom.

By now you have told a few close friends and acquaintances about your new business and maybe you have even found those first few clients. Now it's time to let more people know about your services or products. You probably heard that you need to market your business. You may have already decided that you don't like marketing. This chapter will help you learn how to enjoy this area of business.

I have been around thousands of entrepreneurs, and when the topic of marketing comes up they usually sigh or roll their eyes. Some people who are committed to their business are marketing but they do it as if it's a chore.

Do you enjoy marketing? If not, this chapter will help you change your mind. We will also talk about the place of love in business. When we are controlled by ego and fear, we are not succeeding in business. When we can transcend our ego and fears and live in a state of enlightenment, our business grows.

Understanding Marketing

Let's start with the definition of marketing. On a basic level, according to *Canada Business Network*, "marketing is about determining the value of your product or service and communicating this information to customers".

From this definition you can see that marketing has two parts. The first one is determining the value of your product or service. We already determined what your product or service is and how it relates to your purpose, and in the next chapter we will talk about prices and value. In this chapter, we will focus on the second part of this definition, which is communicating the information about your service or product to your customers.

Another definition I adapted is from Julie Barile, Vice President of eCommerce at Fairway Market: "Marketing is the means by which a business communicates to, connects with, and engages its target audience to convey the value of and ultimately sell its product and services."

This means that marketing is essentially talking about your service to your target audience, and the reason for communicating is to ultimately make the sale.

Julie continues to say that with today's "social media and technology innovations, marketing has become more about building deeper, more meaningful and lasting relationships with your audience" so that they will want to buy your products and services. We have an incredible opportunity right now with social media. It's easy to love marketing when you concentrate on the fact that it is about building relationships with your audience. We humans love bonding and building relationships; therefore, we can love marketing!

Promoting Your Services or Products

For people to buy your product or service, they first need to know it exists. They have to be aware of your service and what it does, then they have to have a positive impression of it, and lastly they need to be convinced that they need it or want it so that they can purchase it. Letting people know about your product or service so they will want to take the next steps and ultimately buy it is called promotion.

Here are some tactics to promote your business to prospective clients:

1) **Traditional advertising:** This consists of television, radio, billboards, newspapers, and magazines. These days we also have online advertising, which is preferred by entrepreneurs with small budgets. Social media is heavily used nowadays because people spend more time on their phones than watching television.

2) **Trade shows**: This is a great way to promote your services. You can choose to be a vendor or exhibitor at trade shows; if you are a good public speaker, you can even present at a trade show. You gain exposure to new people because the organizers gather people there. You will want to let people know about the show as a way to contribute to increasing awareness but the organizers do the heavy lifting to bring people to the show for you. You have to pay to be part of a trade show, plus you have invest in your booth marketing material. You will also have to decide if you will be giving something away to attendees and how you will engage them at your booth.

I like trade shows because they work well for my personality. I do especially well when I am also speaker at the event; this is when I get a few new clients! After trying many forms of promotion, I've discovered that when I'm talking to my prospects in person I can convey who I am and what I offer more effectively.

You will have to decide if trade shows are effective for your business and participating in a few is the best way to know.

3) **Print marketing materials**: Once you've prepared your marketing materials, business cards, fliers, and brochures, you need to distribute them. You can do this by putting up posters around your neighborhood and leaving fliers in strategic places. In addition, you can hand your materials out at networking events. Networking is a very good way to connect with your niche.

Connecting with people is the magic key to marketing.

Handing someone a flier or business card without a connection doesn't do much. To connect, look into that person's eyes when you give them your business card. One of the fears that stop us from marketing is the fear of connection, the fear of being seen.

4) **Direct marketing:** This is when you directly engage people to talk about your product or service. When it's done by telephone, reaching people you don't know, it is called cold-calling. This method is not very popular these days. However, it's a good idea to pick up the phone and talk with people you know about your service or product, or even an upcoming event you are hosting.

Other ways to directly market to your niche are through e-mail and snail mail (post office mail). When you engage with people, ask for their e-mail or mailing address so you can send information. Be sure to first send something valuable to them before you send them a promotion. E-mail is used more these days compared to regular mail because it's easier to get someone's e-mail address. Whenever possible, send something by post mail because these days it's a rarity and it's exciting. People are used to only receiving bills in the mail!

5) **Online advertising:** Having a good website is an excellent way to promote your service. Listing your business in directories is also effective, especially if there are directories for your area if you work locally or in your area of expertise if you work globally. Also try listing in groups and association directories you belong to. For example, if you are a Reiki practitioner and there is a Reiki association, that directory would be a good option for you.

6) **Referrals:** The most rewarding way to promote your services is to get referrals from your existing or past clients. Referrals are the easiest way to get clients since someone who likes you talks about you with another person who trusts them. You need to ask your clients for referrals because sometimes it's not as obvious to them how important this is as it is to

you. Remember to thank them once you receive a referral. Testimonials on your website are also a form of referral.

These are some of the ways to promote your business. You need to determine which approach is right for your business. This depends on your budget and it also depends on your niche's habits. For example, if you are advertising in a newspaper but your niche never reads the newspaper, then this will be a waste of your money. You have to decide where and how it is best for you to promote your business.

As I mentioned, I like to participate in trade shows. I went to some where I had many people stopping by my booth, engaging with me, and purchasing tickets to my event on the spot. I even sold a one-year private coaching package at one of those shows. There was a person who only sat down with me for five minutes before she decided to purchase the one-year package. She and I connected at a deep level and she knew right away that she would benefit from working with me.

I also attended a few shows where I had only a few visitors and that was because the environment was about business but not spirituality and personal development. Not really my niche. One was a business-to-business show. I originally thought it might work because I was addressing my services to businesses. However, they were not purpose-driven businesses and they did not resonate with my offerings. Please note that even if you decide that trade shows are a good way for you to promote your business, you still have to determine which shows are right for you.

Select trade shows where the right people will see your promotion and where you will get the greatest exposure possible for the money spent. Be mindful about the return on investment because not everything that is shiny and flashy will necessarily give you results. Before you jump in and spend hundreds or thousands of dollars, be clear on what results you are expecting. Be sure that you are not just in it for the ego because it is a flashy event or a shiny magazine—you want to ensure that it aligns with who you want to serve, your niche.

At every stage of business, a certain method may be more appropriate than another. Be careful how you spend you marketing and promotional budget, especially at the beginning of your journey. You can effectively market and promote your business with very little money. There is a time for everything, and as the business grows you can explore more expensive methods. Remember that patience is required. Wait for when the time is right.

If something feels like way too much money for you then maybe it's not the right time for such a tactic. Start with something that gives you free exposure, like social media for example. Build strong social media profiles. Show up with a professional photo of yourself on Facebook, LinkedIn, and other social accounts. Develop the story of who you are and what you do, and talk about the topics that are important to you and your niche. Let people know why your business exists; this is how you will build that trust factor with your potential clients.

Finding the Joy in Marketing

Why do we fear marketing? The answer is quite simple: one of our biggest fears as human beings is the fear of rejection. We want to belong, we want to be accepted, and we want to feel good about who we are. When we market ourselves, we feel we are sticking our neck out—we are in a vulnerable position. If people don't click on our post, or people don't register for our event, we feel this is a rejection. This is, of course, painful, and if we associate marketing with rejection then we will want to avoid it in the future.

I used to be sensitive to rejection too. I have been disappointed many times. My blogs used to have an open rate of only 15 percent; this means the number of people who actually clicked to read the full blog was very low. I wondered why I was even bothering to write these blogs if only a few people were reading them. I kept writing because I was committed to my purpose. When I asked how I was selected to be a radio show host, I was told that it was because they looked at my blogs, at what I was teaching, and what I was about. They saw that I was professional and consistent.

This is what I'd like you to remember: you never know who is going to read what you write and when. Put your work out into the world and don't look at what you may perceive as immediate rejection. Know that you are doing what you do because it is your purpose; you are in this for the long run and something good will come out of it eventually.

You can overcome the fear of rejection by connecting with your purpose. Commit to knowing what you are here to do and then do it as long as you are enjoying it. Don't do things if you do not enjoy them: don't write blogs if you do not enjoy writing; don't do presentations if you dislike public speaking. Stay in touch with your potential clients using other methods that work for you. However, if you enjoy writing, then write. If you enjoy being on video, then do videos. Let go of this fear of rejection because sometimes it is just in your mind. You might never know who you inspire and how big of a difference you actually make.

Marketing is not about immediate results. Do your work, put it out there, and let it go. Know that what you are creating now can have ripple effects years after you have done it.

Let go of the fear of rejection and let people know about your product or service. You are following your purpose when someone buys your product or service, and no one can buy if you don't let them know about it.

Negative Thoughts that Prevent You from Loving Marketing

Internalized negative thoughts or beliefs can lead some entrepreneurs to dislike marketing. Have you ever said any of these things to yourself?

Who am I to give advice?

The impostor syndrome can take down any of us—especially when we stretch and strive to take our business to the next level. It's especially prevalent when you are starting a new business.

Another variation of this limiting belief is "how can I tell people I'm a healer if I'm not fully healed?" This is what you need to know to transcend this limitation: no one is fully healed; no one is fully enlightened. Healing is a continuous process; as we progress through life, we discover more things we need to heal, learn, and understand.

We can only heal so much on our own. At some point we need to practice our work in order to heal ourselves further. Our clients provide examples that allow us to go deeper. We all have blind spots. It is easy to heal what we know needs to be healed, but after we deal with the obvious we get into that place where we don't see what's missing.

When a client comes to you, if you are in a state of enlightenment you have put your ego aside to be in full service to them. This way you become really receptive to the voice of angels, Universe, God, nature, or whatever you call the higher power. Through this receptivity you also get messages and healing for yourself. When you heal others you are also being healed if you stay in balance.

It's really important to get this so you don't stay home hiding until you are fully healed because that is not the way to get better at your work. Be courageous enough to put yourself out there. Entrepreneurship is a very good way to enlightenment because it will bring us what needs to be healed, and it will bring us the exact clients we need to grow. Doing our work makes us push the boundaries of our comfort zone.

If you are afraid of marketing, ask yourself: What do I need to heal to be able to like marketing? What do I need to heal in order to send the e-mail and ask for that referral? What do I need to heal in order to post a picture of me in a networking group? You probably need to heal that fear of being seen. When you are an entrepreneur in your own business, you can directly see the results of your work; this is a big blessing because you can see what else needs to be healed.

If you tell yourself you do not have what it takes to give others advice, remember that what you have to say is valuable. No one in this world has said what you say exactly like you say it. Some believe that there is nothing special about what they have to say because it has been said before. Indeed, there is nothing new under the sun but it has never been said the way you are saying it!

As I was writing the theory part of this chapter, I kept thinking that this has already been said in other books on marketing. I myself learned marketing from my mentors. Who am I to even write about marketing? The truth is that although I learned marketing tactics from others, I came to my own conclusions about how those tactics should be applied. I have had my own epiphanies about how to turn my reluctance for marketing into something I enjoy doing. What I write now is my understanding, my explanation; it is uniquely mine. I did not invent marketing but I understand how to apply it. I understood what is needed to get over my fears. When I taught those principles to my clients they had a change of heart too. I'm sharing this with you so you can benefit as well.

Say what you have to say, give the advice you have to give. Somebody might have heard a similar message many times, but it is when you say it that something clicks, something shifts, and something comes to light. Maybe your clients needed to hear what you say in that moment, the way you said it. Let go of that fear of not feeling competent and share your message. Your clients need to hear it from you.

My expertise is common sense.

You may feel that there is nothing special about your expertise and you may want to hold back sharing it with people because you think everybody knows what you know. For example, I created the Business-Start Up 21 Points Checklist to start a business (you can

download this at EntrepreneurEnlightenment.com/EE1Resources).
I really thought that it was no big deal. It's just a bullet-point list of
how to start your business. I thought it was common sense until I
sent it to my clients and they told me how great it was. They told me
it motivated them to make progress and know where they are in the
process–that sounds like more than just common sense.

Your expertise may seem common sense to you because you've
done it and lived it for so many years, but it is not common sense
to someone who is just starting out. Your expertise is revolutionary
to people who are starting their journey on the path that you have
already traveled.

No one wants what I have to offer.

Another negative belief preventing you from loving marketing is
the fear that no one wants what you have to offer or that no one will
pay for your services. And guess what, you will never know if they
will until you market yourself and put your offer out there.

When you promote your offer you will get feedback from potential
clients and you will know if you need to tweak it. The next time you
put that offer out it will be improved and will resonate better with
your potential customers. Don't be afraid of marketing; let people
know about your services or products!

I am not an extrovert.

Some entrepreneurs think that they cannot be successful at
marketing because they are introverts or not good public speakers.
This is a topic I address with all my clients: no matter your personality,
there is a way for everyone to be successful. Everyone has the perfect
skills for their purpose and everyone has the opportunity to succeed
no matter their inclinations. Not all successful entrepreneurs are good
speakers. You have to find your way of marketing your business by
figuring out what comes naturally to you. If you are a good writer,

then write. If you are a good speaker, then speak. If you look good on video, then do videos. If you are good at analyzing data, then issue a report. Don't be stuck on what you are not good at; look at what you are good at and do that.

I don't want to take advantage of people.

This negative belief is probably the most feared and prevents many entrepreneurs from marketing effectively. Some entrepreneurs feel that if they promote their business they will be like a sleazy used-car salesman. Thinking there is something bad about promoting and selling prevents many from greatness. Are you really trying to take advantage of people or trying to deceive them? You are in a purpose-driven business because you want to help people. You cannot help if you do not promote; you cannot help if you do not tell people about your service.

I'll give you a visual representation: Imagine your potential client is walking down the street, and right in front of them is a big pothole they can fall in. Your service is to cover the pothole for them. If you do not stop them and say "hey potential client, let me offer you my services because you are just about to fall into the pothole", then you are not helping.

What do you do if they are already in the pothole and your service is to lift them up? It's selfish to leave them there because you are frozen by the fear of marketing your business. How is it possible to walk by, see their predicament, and say nothing? You have a duty to tell them what is available to them; you have a duty to offer them your service. If they want to stay in the pothole, that's fine—at least you know you have done your part by offering your services.

The Place of Love in Business

In order to be open to marketing, the first thing you need to do is love your product or service. In his memoir *I Can See Clearly Now*, Wayne W. Dyer describes how he loved each and every one of his books. He loved his books so much that he wanted everyone to have a copy. This was true even before he was famous. He bought 4,000 copies of his first book, *Your Erroneous Zones*, just to make it successful. He put the books in the back of his truck and went to sell them at the market. He loved what he wrote, and he believed that everyone should have this knowledge because it would help them. He thought his book would help people live better lives. He also loved his first movie so much that he always had copies in his pocket to give away to people he met on his walks.

Love Your Service or Product

In order to love your service or product, you need to review how it has helped you. As we heal and grow we forget where we started and how far we have come. I am guilty of that and I am always looking for what is next. I forget that 15 years ago I would suffer for months because I felt rejected and today when that happens it only stings for a few minutes and then it's gone. That's progress! In order to love your service or product, review how it has helped you and what is possible now in your life because of what you have discovered through it.

To gain confidence in your service or product and in yourself, make a ritual by reviewing your testimonials. Reminisce about your past clients; remember how they were when they first walked into your practice and how they were when they left. Understand what other people have said about working with you and what results they experienced. Know those benefits well and remind yourself of the value that you have to offer; this will help you market your business successfully.

Love Your Customers Enough to Market Your Business

You have to love people enough to transcend your fears and confidently present what you have to offer. If you are good at marketing, people will buy from you and your service or product will enhance their lives.

You've got to love people enough to want to support them; this is the key element to loving marketing. If you say you don't like marketing, it's like saying you don't like to help people. I know this is not true because if you are in a purpose-driven business, you love people and you want to help them. Maybe this distinction makes it easier for you to market your business and put your offer out there.

Love Yourself Enough to Market Your Business

Maya Angelou says:

"Success is liking yourself, liking what you do, and liking how you do it."

When this is true for you, you are in an enlightened state. When you are aligned with your purpose, your business succeeds. You are probably asking what liking yourself has to do with marketing. When you don't like yourself, it is hard for you to put yourself out there, right?

When I was doing the radio show, I would make it a point to listen to the episode once it become available on replay. I get pleasantly surprised how well I do on air. I really do like my shows and my videos. Maybe this sounds like vanity but it was not always like this. The first time I spoke into a microphone, and I still vividly remember that day, I was scared of my voice. Through my personal transformation work, I came to love myself and my voice.

When I listen to my previous shows or videos and I find the information I'm providing valuable, it gives me the drive to do more of it. If you look at your videos and only concentrate on the negative aspects, then of course you will not want to do more of them. If you don't love marketing, dig deep within to find out if you like yourself. And if you don't, take the steps needed to embrace who you are.

Love Your Business Enough to Market It Well

Maya Angelou's quote on success also mentions liking *how you do it*. This is very important because if you don't like how you do your business then you will not want more clients; therefore, you will not want to market it because you will not want it to grow. Set up your business in a way that suits you.

If you feel your business is a drag, or you get bogged down by how many things you have to do or how early you have to wake up, you will have issues becoming successful. Arrange your business in a way that is enjoyable for you.

A client of mine really enjoys traveling. However, when she booked too many in-person client meetings, she was not able to travel as much as she wanted to. As a result, she was not marketing enough and as a result she did not have enough clients. We introduced Skype sessions, so now she can travel and keep up with her business at the same time.

Embracing the Love

I will leave you with a few thoughts about the place of love in business:

1. Loving yourself is number one. This is your business and your purpose. You are here to serve a purpose. You are here to be uniquely you, to be the quirky you, the eccentric you, the weird you that you are, and this is exactly who you need to be. Without you in your life there would be no purpose. You are your number one asset: the most valuable asset you have in your business.

2. Loving what you do is number two. Loving your service and knowing how it has helped you and how it helped other people is very important in order to have success in business.
3. Loving people is number three. Loving your current and potential clients and wanting to share with them what you have discovered is essential for marketing your business with ease.

A good practice for when you are about to sit down and create your marketing materials is to connect your heart with the heart of one of your favorite clients. Choose someone you feel you have helped the most. I have some testimonials from people who say "you saved my life!" Knowing this helps me want to reach more people. You may have awesome testimonials too. Connect with one of those people with whom you feel a deep bond. Take a deep breath and go tell the world what you have to offer.

CHAPTER 7

Release the Fears of Receiving Money for Your Service

In this chapter, we'll explore the true meaning of money. We'll look at what fears show up when we receive money for our services, and how we can release those fears to easily accept money with an open heart and thrive in business.

I'd like to start with a quote about enlightenment:

"You can search throughout the entire Universe for someone who is more deserving of your love and affection and that person is not to be found anywhere. You yourself as much as anybody in the entire Universe deserve your love and affection." Buddha

When you decide to honor who you are and give yourself your love and affection, you quickly progress on your spiritual path to an enlightened state.

When you have your own business, it is critical to give yourself love and affection, especially if you are a service provider. Nurturing yourself and loving yourself ensures that you have energy to give to your clients and help your business succeed.

As a service provider, you are probably kind-hearted; you started your business because you want to help people. You decided to put yourself out there despite the many battles you had to fight with your ego and all of the fears you had to transcend. You have a kind heart, and that heart's love and kindness has to include you.

On a call with one of my clients we came up with a great statement: nobody needs you more than you. It rings true, doesn't it? When you are in good shape, in good health, in good mental focus, and in a good emotional state, you can easily give from the goodness of your heart. You don't have to make an effort to serve your clients. You become a much better service provider and your business grows when you have love and affection for yourself.

I know you are tempted to be impatient with yourself or criticize yourself when things don't work out the way you want. I know because I'm tempted too. When this happens I remind myself that everything is in divine order and give myself a break. Be good to yourself and your business will be good to you.

In the last chapter we talked about marketing, how to enjoy the process, and how to bring love into business. Going from marketing to sales is only a tiny step. When marketing, you let people know about your business, you share what you do, and you engage with your target audience. The ultimate purpose of marketing is to sell your product or service.

In order for people to buy what you offer, they need to be aware that your service exists. Next, they need to have a positive impression of it. People have to feel that they know, like, and trust you. They also need to be convinced that they have a need for what you offer to solve a problem or give them a benefit they are after.

In marketing, you talk with people in general; in sales, you are down to one person or a small group of people. Now you've got to talk to them in particular to make the sale, to ask for the money. This is when it really starts to get difficult for most entrepreneurs.

Let's say someone found out about your service and they send you an e-mail saying they are interested in your business. You might feel some fears coming up. It's easier to hide behind the computer and send e-mails or post on social media, but now you need to talk with someone directly. You need to close the sale and you will have to face your fears.

Selling a service seems harder than selling a product because it's as if you have to sell "you". When this is combined with not feeling worthy or deserving of money, selling becomes almost impossible.

To illustrate this point, here's is an edited transcript from an interaction with a live caller from the radio show. This is what Samantha said when she called:

"I think where I have a problem with the fear of selling my services is that I'm not selling something tangible, you know? If I was selling something that I knitted or that I cooked, I'd have no problem saying 'hey, this is a great thing I made and I really think you should have it and you obviously need to pay me for it'. But when it's something that's coming from inside of me, that isn't something that I can put in my hand and give to somebody, I have a problem asking for money."

This is why it feels harder to sell a service then selling a product: it feels like you're selling yourself. You're selling something that's inside of you, as Samantha expressed.

When I was in my corporate role, I was very good at sales. I proposed and negotiated projects, and as a result I raised my department's business from about $1.2 million to $7 million–a 600 percent increase! When I started my coaching business, I thought to myself: how hard can it be? I know how to talk; I know how to convince people; I know how to sell! After a few attempts to make sales, I realized that it is actually very hard because it felt like I was selling me.

In my corporate job I had a big team. I would go to our clients and say our engineers are brilliant, our projects are great, and we've delivered these projects successfully in the past. This was easy for me. I was so proud of the team and what we were doing. In my own business, I felt I had to go to a potential client and say "hey, hire me because I'm so good". This is hard, right?

Making the sale is especially hard if you are introverted. It can also be difficult if you were taught not to toot your own horn because that was not acceptable behavior.

Samantha says, "Yes, absolutely, it was the opposite. It was how good I wasn't."

When you sell a service such as coaching, Reiki healing, or other therapies and healing modalities, although you are spending time with your client, what you do is not tangible. This makes it harder to sell. If you are a Reiki practitioner, sometimes your client won't know if the Reiki energy actually flows through them. This is the doubt you have to overcome because Reiki energy is not tangible. I feel this is why so many practitioners are stuck in the dollars-for-hours business model because they feel they can at least put a dollar value on their time and that makes their service more tangible.

Selling Services with Ease

Here is a process that makes it easier to sell your services.

1. Focus on your potential customer

Selling a service becomes easier when you focus the attention on the other person. Understand your potential client's needs, ask questions, and focus on their pain or desire. Identify how you can help them relieve that pain or achieve that desire.

I've seen entrepreneurs at networking events talking about themselves when they make that initial contact. They say I do this and I do that, trying to impress their potential customer because they are self-conscious or nervous. The more they talk, the more the other person shuts down. When we try to prove ourselves, we put pressure on the other person to approve of us. When people feel pressured to do something they are not sure they can do, they distance themselves energetically.

Instead of talking about yourself, ask questions to understand the other person better. You can do this either when you meet someone in person, or when you meet someone over the phone or on a video call. You can ask direct questions like, "what is it that you're searching for?". This way, they are talking and you're not selling. If your questions are guiding them properly, then they will be talking themselves into the awareness that they might need your services.

When you focus on understanding the other person first, you don't waste time trying to sell in case they are not a good fit and you avoid unnecessary rejection. Not everybody is your client. If you remember my story with my hairdresser neighbor, you can save yourself some embarrassment!

One of my clients works with soccer moms. When she goes to a game, she meets about 20 moms there. She asked me what to do in that situation because she feels nervous every time she meets those moms. I told her that not all 20 moms are her potential clients–only two of them may fit the bill. Instead of going up to the group and nervously talking about her services, it's better to gauge who fits her ideal client profile and approach them separately. Asking questions is the way to find out if people are open to your services. If you feel that you understand them and have a good connection, you can start to share what you offer.

When I go to expos I always put angel cards on my table. This is so people who are spirituality inclined are attracted to stop and talk with me. It also gives those who are not into those methods a reason to pass by, and this saves us all time and energy.

2. Talk about your clients and the results of your work

Instead of talking about yourself and how great you are, it's much more elegant to talk about your clients who had similar problems and the results they got by working with you. This flows easily after you understand your potential client and their problems.

Samantha says, "Yeah, I think this is what I need to do. I haven't had any paying clients per se, but I've coached people for years. People have always told me I am good at doing this and it's partly why I went into coaching. People felt that this is something that I would be really good at. I think that I will reach out to those people who've encouraged me so much and ask them to write testimonials for me focusing on something that I did for them and helped them get through. And then I will have something tangible in my head. I will have these testimonials which are tangible and maybe that will help me to push myself forward. I think that's probably a good start."

This is a good strategy. If you haven't had clients yet there must be a reason you decided to do what you do, and maybe there were people encouraging you too. You can share with your potential client that you've started your business because people have told you that you were skilled in this area. At the beginning when you haven't had paying clients to give you testimonials, you can use what your friends and family say about what you are good at. Instead of saying "look at me" and "how great am I", you can say "look at the great things other people say about me". This is much easier on you and feels less intimidating for the person listening.

You need to be mindful of the fact that when you try to sell something and you feel uneasy or self-conscious, the person on the other end of the conversation feels uncomfortable too. They foresee the end of the discussion as something unpleasant. They will either have to reject you or accept what you are selling without being completely sure they need it. As much as we don't like rejection, we also don't like to reject others–probably because we know it's painful.

3. Close the sale!

When you feel you understand this potential client's needs, and you've shared the results that your other clients have achieved by working with you, then it's your duty to ask for the sale.

My favorite way of asking is: "would you like that?" Let's say we talked about this client who suffered with this and got that as a result.

I would say: would you like that for yourself? Instead of asking him to hire me, I ask him if he would like to get the results we discussed.

The reason why you have to ask for the sale is because maybe this person desperately needs your services. Maybe you can change the course of their life and the courses of the lives of the other people in their life.

You have to care enough to want to relieve their pain. A strategy to make it easy for you to enter the close-the-sale conversation is to put your hand on your heart and think about the potential client. Feel love coming into your heart from theirs.

I asked Samantha to do this exercise and see if she feels the love. This is what she said: "Absolutely. I mean, the things that I would like to help people with are things that I've been through myself that have knocked me down. I can see people who are knocked down and need that helping hand to come back up again, absolutely. I want to lift them up, to help them. I can hold their hand on the path, so absolutely. That would be one of my strengths."

Why Do We Fear Sales?

When it comes to making the sale, there are several fears that show up that we have to overcome.

Fear that we are not worthy

Taking money from someone raises one of our deepest fears: that we are not worthy. This fear is one of the biggest blocks to making the monetary exchange. We need to transcend this fear, and we can do it when we get out of our head and get into our heart instead. We need to be willing to be of service to others. When a client needs your service, you have to be willing to take their money. If you're not, then they're not going to have the services they need and they are not going to solve their problem. Some practitioners give away their service for free, but the client does not fully benefit because they won't fully value the gift they are receiving. For someone to commit to change, they need to invest.

The question of worthiness comes out when we decide what to charge for our services, and especially when we need to explain why that is the right price. For this, we have to go back and review how our service has helped others. We will go deeper into pricing in the next chapter.

I want you to think about your first sale and answer the question: what do I need to shift in me in order to accept money with more ease? Without accepting money, you are not going to be able to help people. By not accepting money, you will not have a business for very long, and you might have to go work for somebody else instead of following your purpose. This will not be good for you, not helpful for the client, and definitely not beneficial for the greater good.

Fear that we don't matter

One major desire we have as humans is to feel that we matter— that we are important. This is why we deeply fear rejection. When we are rejected, we feel put down. We talked about the fear of rejection in the last chapter as this fear prevents us from marketing effectively. When we have to close the sale, the chances of rejection are 50/50. You are in front of your potential customer and you either make the sale, or you don't and face rejection.

Now, it is up to you how you interpret that rejection.

If you interpret the rejection as something personal and you proceed to tell yourself that you are not good enough, or that you did not present the offer well, or that what you have to offer has no value, then yes: rejection is hard! This kind of thinking will make you sweat when you have to close a sale and your enthusiasm for entrepreneurship will quickly diminish.

On the other hand, if you take the rejection as something external and you tell yourself that the other person might not have needed what you offered, they could not afford it, it is not the right time, or they would not give themselves permission to have it, then you will not suffer and you will continue to attempt making sales.

I find the people who need it most don't want to hire a coach because they think they should be able to do it on their own. I have heard this excuse so many times! I've also heard about some of those same people having given up. This makes me sad.

When you continue attempting to make sales and get better and better at it, you will eventually succeed and your business will grow.

Fear of not being able to deliver on the promise

Let's resume our call with Samantha.

Irina: Samantha, can you imagine that you have a sales conversation with a potential client. They are ready to buy and want to know how much you charge. They want to pay you. Can you imagine that and tell me what fears come up?

Samantha: Oh, I guess the fears would be just that now they've placed their confidence in me and that I'm not going to be able to live up to what I've just sold them. I'm worried I'll sell them a car without an engine.

This is the fear of not being able to deliver on the promise. In order to alleviate this fear, you can keep the money they give you in the bank. Don't spend it and know that if by any chance you cannot deliver on your promise, you will give them the money back.

Do this especially for the first few clients, until you gain more confidence in yourself and what you can deliver. Remember the worst that can happen is that you will have to refund somebody their money. Be willing to refund the money even if you lose out.

For example, some workshop facilitators say they will give the money back if by lunchtime the customer is not satisfied with the value of the course. They have already bought the food and rented the room, but they are still willing to give the money back. Business is a game, sometimes we make money, and sometimes we lose money. It's all good as long as we move forward and grow.

When you offer a money-back guarantee, it might make it easier for you to sell and easier for the customer to buy. You give the customer a way out if they do not like it and they feel they are not risking much by buying. It's a win-win situation!

Another caller from the radio show, Heather, brought up an interesting point: "I'm facing a challenge with being able to find sales opportunities with the child-free women community. I'm pretty much selling more happiness and freedom to them. It's hard to say 'hey, do you want more happiness and freedom?' Some of them think 'oh, I didn't even know I could be happier.' Others haven't put the pieces together in their lives yet. They are not even realizing they need a coach or a support system for that. So, it's not 'I'll help you with your business' or 'I'll help you with parenting your kids'. It feels like a hard sell for me. How do I actually get them into that dialogue or conversation?"

The problem Heather faces is that what she is selling is not tangible. To solve this problem, she needs to make what she is selling tangible. Sounds complicated, right? I'll tell you what I did. When you work with me, you become more authentic, more empowered, and more connected. What does it mean to be more authentic? Authenticity isn't something you can hold in your hand. I developed a questionnaire to help people determine their level of authenticity. It contains probing questions like: when you make decisions, do you look at others for approval? I created this self-assessment tool and I ask people to send me the results before coming on our initial call. If they scored low in authenticity, then we know there is room for improvement. This is my way of measuring the level of authenticity in a way that is tangible. (Get a copy at EntrepreneurEnlightenment. com/EE1Resources)

Heather can apply this tactic as well. If she can find a way to measure the level of happiness of her niche, then selling the solution through coaching to support increasing that level becomes obvious. Some examples of questions for Heather's audience are: Have you dreamed of writing your book but can't start on it? Have you felt like you don't belong? What aspect of your life needs more joy? Heather can ask her questions in a way that reinforces her method of creating happiness for her clients. Happiness is a generic term; clients can be happy when they're healthy; they can be happy when they achieve something. Heather needs to define happiness for them.

For the child-free women that Heather caters to, a sense of community or circle of support may be what they are after.

> Irina: Heather, you can ask questions like: Do you still feel guilty for making the choice to be child free? Do you still feel worried that you are missing something? You can explain your service and how you help them achieve more happiness. You have to go one level deeper.

> Heather: Okay, that makes a lot of sense, Irina. I feel that happiness and freedom for child-free women is becoming clearer. They come into their own truth, their own personal power. How much are they really living their truth?

> Irina: Yes, because a lot of people live in hiding! Maybe that's how you are going to help them when you say it's about freedom and happiness. You're going to show them how to really feel they can be who they are without feeling they have to fit the mold. For example, being able to play volleyball in front of their house, without worrying that others might think they are childish. I think that's what happiness and freedom is.

We refine the results of our work as we discover more about what people working with us experience. Your clients will tell you some of the results you provide. Sometimes they will be surprising. For example, I'm told I bring people peace, and I don't know how I do that! Perhaps it is my inner peace and acceptance of everyone who wants to grow. One of my clients said that she felt as if she was naked after our sessions were completed because she didn't feel my energy around her anymore. Some of the things you offer are not tangible, but you can still bring them into the sales conversation directly or through customer testimonials.

Fear that the person who gives us money will have authority over us

There is an underlying fear that the person who gives us money has authority over us and we become responsible to them after the exchange.

At work, people have a tendency to fear their boss. In business, the client becomes that person we tend to fear.

I remember the first time that someone handed me their credit card for coaching services. I was at the front of our store and my hands shook badly when trying to put their credit card through the machine. I wonder why. When I worked in the corporate sector I received my paycheck every two weeks and my hand never shook. Why is it so hard to take money from a person who is physically in front of you?

When you take money from someone, you feel that somehow that person starts to have power over you. Most times this fear is subconscious. People fear their boss because they feel the boss can alter their life. This can be in positive ways if they get a raise or in negative ways if they get fired. Some people transfer this fear to clients in their business. They feel the client is now like their boss.

This is where another fear comes in: what if we cannot please them? We feel as if our happiness depends on our ability to please this person. But what do you do if you cannot please them?

Remember this: whether someone is happy or not is entirely their choice. When you connect your worth with your ability to please someone you always lose. Humans are not consistent in what makes them happy or unsatisfied. One day something makes them happy and another day the same thing can bother them.

I have had clients who have said things like "you saved my life", "I love you", and "you changed my life". The same person later runs into some difficulties and they tell me: "I don't think your coaching is working for me, and I want to quit". This does happen.

How do you transcend this fear of not being able to please your client? You need to detach yourself from your clients' moods. Take their feedback into account to improve your services, but know that it is not your responsibility to make them happy or even to make them obtain the result that they had signed up for.

You have a responsibility to them but not a responsibility for them. See the difference? You are responsible for delivering the services as you promised when they signed up with you. You have the responsibility to be professional and do your work in good faith. But you are not responsible for their happiness or for their results; they have to do the work. There are two people in this transaction, not just you.

Remember that if it is warranted, you can always give somebody their money back. I have done this a few times. Fairly early in my coaching career, I had a client who was skipping sessions, not coming prepared, and not doing the work. I felt frustrated every time I had a session with her. I figured that there was no way she would be happy with the work we were doing. She came to the calls unhappy. One day I said to her, "I don't think this is working for you. I don't think I'm the right coach for you. How about I give you your money back and maybe you go and find somebody else who can support you." She sure was a sweetheart because she only wanted half of the money back; she said that she did make some progress with me. Bless her heart; she was fair to me. Even if she wanted all the money back it was better for me to lose that money than put up with the suffering

I was going through when I had her sessions. The story has a funny twist because when I went to my former husband, who was then in charge of accounting, and told him to refund her money, there was no money in our account! We had to borrow it to make the refund. Still, it felt authentic to give her money back and I felt empowered after. It needed to be done.

I caution you not to give money back with ease, because this is not how business is done. But know that if needed, you have that way out. Your client is not your authority. If you mistakenly think that you have to please your client, then you will not be doing a good job being of service to them.

Sometimes I joke with my clients and I tell them I'm not here to please them. As a coach I have to dig out uncomfortable truths. Sometimes I put my clients on the spot at events to help them shift, to help them become more of who they are. I call them out on excuses. My focus in not on "pleasing" them in the moment but helping them get the results they are after in the long run.

When you see your client as your authority figure, you're losing your ability to provide your service. You are the authority. You are leading them to get the results; you know what needs to be done. Release this fear of your client being your boss. You don't have to obey them.

The best way to position yourself with your client is at an equal level. They are not above you because they pay you, and you are not above them because you are the teacher or the expert. You are equal. You are a team; you are partners and you came together to solve a problem or to achieve a dream. This is the best position to be in; it's the most loving and balanced position.

I hope you are able to transcend those fears now that you understand them. You need to find a way to sell your services because this is how you make business. This is how you follow your purpose.

The Role of Money

Money is energy. When you provide a service or a product, your client gives you money in exchange. This balances the energy between you two.

Some spiritual entrepreneurs have an underlying limiting thought that money is bad. Money is neither good nor bad. Money can be used for good things or bad things. Money helps you be more of who you are.

To make it easy for you to receive money for your services, answer these questions: What would you do with more money? What will more money make possible for you? How will you having more money improve the lives of your future clients? How will more money help you help the world?

In my case, more money will allow me to eradicate the effects of abuse and to raise awareness so cases of abuse decrease considerably. I established Irinuca – Child Innocence Foundation to help abused children ages 12 to 20 evolve from being emotionally traumatized to becoming truly free, empowered, and confident in their future and know how to achieve economic self-sufficiency.

When you have more money, you will create more. You will be able to support a cause you care about.

You are making this world a better place first through fulfilling your purpose and you can do so when you make good money in your business.

Making more and more money in your business is also important. When kind and loving people like you have more money, more kindness spreads into the world.

When you think about what you will create with more money, selling your services becomes easier.

CHAPTER 8

How to Price Your Service Right

In the first few chapters, we covered the internal work you need to do before you take your business out into the world. We explored how you can align your business with your authentic self and your purpose, and how you can thrive by being who you are and doing what you love.

We then talked about getting out into the world with your services, and how to enjoy marketing and sales. We discovered how to release the fear of rejection, the fear of criticism, and the fear of not being good enough. We talked about how to easily accept money for your services.

This chapter takes it one step further: we'll talk about how to price your services right. I will dispel the myth that you have to charge your worth, and explain why it is not good for business. We'll also explore how to relieve money pressures so you can close more sales.

Selling a service seems harder than selling a product because it's as if you have to sell yourself. The solution, as we covered previously, is to sell the results of your service and to focus on the benefits your clients get from your service. The next logical question is what to charge, right? You might be tempted to look around and see what other people in your industry charge as a way to establish your prices. If you defined your service as unique, then following what others charge might not be feasible.

There is some general motivational advice that says you should charge your worth. I completely disagree with this. First and foremost, your worth cannot be measured; your worth is actually priceless. How you establish your price is a business decision. It is a positioning strategy and it has to fit with the types of clients you want to attract and the value the clients get as a result. There are businesses who charge on the low end, such as Walmart, and there are businesses who charge a premium price like Rolls Royce.

> *Pricing is a positioning strategy—it is not about your worth.*

Pricing is a business decision that is related to the stage of business you are in. At the beginning of your business journey, you will want to have lower prices because you will want to get clients, gain experience, and build a reputation. Once you feel comfortable, you can increase your prices. On the other hand, be careful not to start with prices that are too low for your industry. If you start with rock-bottom prices, be sure to put a limit on how many clients you will serve at that level and then move your prices up. If you start too low, it might take you longer to build your business up. Start with a price that is reasonable for your industry, for your expertise, and for you clients. You can call the low starting price an introductory price and put a time limit on it.

Pricing is also influenced by your vision of what you want to create. In my business, when I priced the Entrepreneur Enlightenment Academy group program, I decided on a price lower than the industry standard. My vision is to build a community of supportive entrepreneurs. I believe that in a group, you and your business can grow with more ease. In order to create the community and make it self-sustainable, I decided to make it affordable for people to join. At the same time, the price was high enough to attract committed individuals who wanted to invest in their success because they were ready to put in the work.

To decide how to price your service, ask yourself these questions: What are my core values? What do I want to achieve through my business? What is my priority right now? You might have a 10-year vision, but for now focus on the stage you are currently in. Figure out what your clients' core values are, and align your prices accordingly.

I know there are concepts out there which say that you have to charge more. And maybe you succumb to this pressure and decide to set your prices higher. I want to caution you: it is very important that you feel comfortable with your prices. To be an enlightened entrepreneur is to work with both spiritual principles and practical business strategies. Increasing your price might be a business strategy to help you make more money, but if you are not comfortable with that price, your energy will be out of alignment and you will not be able to make the sale.

You have to be very comfortable with the price to make the sale with ease. When you convey the price of your service, your energy has to show that you know you are providing a good value. Your customers need to feel that they are getting great value in return for their investment. If you think your product or service is too expensive, you will not be able to sell it to anyone else. You have to like the price.

The first person to buy your service is you.

How to Calculate Your Worth

Although I cautioned you to not be tempted to buy into the myth that you need to charge your worth, it is still a good exercise to calculate how much you have invested in order for you to be able to deliver your service. This will prevent you from keeping your prices low for too long. People who keep their prices low for too long usually lack self-confidence, and this exercise will provide some perspective.

When you want to get a job working for someone else, you write a resume that shows your experience and why you are the right person for this position. In business, no one asks you about your resume. However, it is still a good idea to have one even if it's only for you.

In addition to listing your experience in your entrepreneurial resume, you can also calculate the value of investment you have made to complete all the degrees and qualifications you have attained. Then add how much time you have invested to get good at what you do. Even if you have a college or university degree that might not be directly linked to what you offer now, this is still an investment on your part and it is still an asset. You learned how to solve problems, how to absorb and synthesize information, and how to think critically. This is all useful no matter what you do.

This calculation helps you understand why you decided to charge a certain price. How much have you actually invested in your training to come to this point where you can offer this service? If you need an office and special equipment to deliver your service, be sure to include a portion for depreciation, maintenance, and utilities.

As I said at the beginning, don't confuse this calculation with charging your worth. Why not? Let's say you determine your so-called "worth" and then you try to make the sale. You tell your client you arrived at this price based on what you're worth, and your client thinks it is far too expensive. This will hurt your ego, won't it? It will feel as though your client doesn't see your worth.

When you attach your product or service price to your worth, you are influenced by your ego and you can get your feelings hurt. It's possible you may not even want to call this potential client again. You might not want to follow up because you feel they don't understand your value. You will lose out on a sale because of your ego.

When we are in a state of enlightenment, we understand that there is a spiritual purpose for our business. We know our purpose is to serve and to help others. We know that our ego has to be put to the side. When you disconnect your price from your worth, this becomes much easier.

When somebody says that your service is too expensive, this could be because of a few different reasons not connected to your worth:
- They may not understand what they get for that price.
- They may not feel they will receive a good return on investment.
- They may be under financial stress and cannot afford anyone's service.

This is why it is important not to take rejection personally. Either you have to communicate the value you're providing more effectively, or you have to accept that the client is at a stage of their journey where they are not ready for what you have to offer.

Don't let your ego make you lose a sale and the possibility to help this person. What if you are meant to work with this client, if not now at least in the future? You have to follow up with people many times, even twelve times if that's what it takes.

Know that somehow the Universe has connected the two of you, and maybe there is a greater purpose for that connection. It's true that we are not meant to work with everybody, and maybe that connection is meant to be short lived. Maybe you help those people in an indirect way, perhaps when they read an article that you write or a post on Facebook. Maybe they show up to a webinar you offer. Maybe that brief discussion was enough for them to shift towards what they needed.

If you feel in your heart that there is something there, don't let your ego stop you from following up. You never know how you can be the light in somebody's life. Remember this: you need to love people enough to follow up with them.

What you charge is a business decision and a positioning strategy. It's better not to associate your worth with how much your service costs.

Exchanging Energy in Business

Doing business together is an exchange of energy. People give you money, and you give them your service or product.

Some spiritual entrepreneurs have difficulty charging for their services because they feel they charge for love and that should be free. It is! You charge your clients for your skill, your knowledge, and your experience. You are not charging for love. Love is free and is on top of everything else you offer.

If you have difficulty charging for you services because you feel you are channeling Universal wisdom or energy and that should be free as it is available to anyone, know why you are charging. You are charging for preparing yourself to be a clear vessel and for the time you took to learn your modality and to hone in your skills to understand and discern the information.

One of my clients was just starting her business and was approached by someone to give her a healing session. My client didn't know what to charge. She asked me if it would be appropriate for her to tell her customer to pay whatever they felt was reasonable. I said no.

There are a few reasons why this is not a good strategy. One reason is that you are the leader. Your client does not know what is involved for you to do the work. They don't understand how much time you've spent, how much training you have acquired, or how much experience you have.

If the customer gives you a lower number than the one you have in your head, then your ego will be bruised and you might feel offended. If you employ this technique, it can also mean that you are insecure and they might lose confidence in your ability to deliver the service. The placebo effect was studied at length: the confidence that people have in you is an important factor for the success they obtain by using your service or product.

It is not your client's job to recognize your value. It is your job to own your value and to help your client see the value they are receiving in exchange for their investment.

Another question I often get is whether it's a good idea to put prices up on the website so potential clients can see them up front. I don't recommend having prices on your website or sending them out in an e-mail. The buying decision is an emotional one.

When your potential client sees a number written down on a screen or piece of paper, it has no emotion associated with it. Sometimes the very people who need support are the people who find excuses for why they shouldn't buy the service. They are usually achievers; they think they should be able to do it by themselves. They're usually people who give themselves a hard time, thinking they should not need someone to hold their hand through their problem.

When they see the price written down, they may think they cannot afford it. They may not understand the value. On the other hand, when you connect with someone on a call or in person, they connect with your energy and they feel your love and care.

When you connect with a potential client, you ask them what they want to achieve, what is stopping them from achieving that, and why it is important to them to move forward. When you ask those questions, you are connecting on an emotional level. Through the answers to those questions, you can also evaluate whether you can support them. This is so you don't take somebody's money if you feel they will not fully benefit from what you have to offer.

I know that not everyone would enjoy coaching with me because my style is to go deep rather fast and have people take action quickly. I'm an activator. There are people who will benefit more from a counseling-style session where they can talk for hours and analyze the past. People who benefit from working with me are open to spiritual growth and personal development while they grow their business. If someone is searching just for a business coach, my teachings are not right for them.

The same goes for you: some people will like your style while others won't. It is important to check if you and your potential client are aligned. If you both reach the conclusion that you would like to work together, share your price and explain the benefits of working together. Make the proposal.

Once you've shared the price, keep quiet to see what they say. Be sure to not oversell. If they don't say anything, ask them how the price feels. If they say it's expensive, resist the temptation to defend your price or to discount it. A better strategy is to reiterate why this service was important to them in the first place. See if you can compare the price of them not achieving their goal with the price they would pay to get your service or product. Try to put your price in perspective.

Once they have agreed to your price, you need to ask them how they would like to pay. I have seen many of my clients doing the happy dance thinking they got a new client and then waiting for days for the payment to come through. You only have a new client once someone pays you and money is in the bank. Make sure to close the deal right away. There isn't a better time to close the deal than in the moment when your customer is emotionally engaged with you.

When quantifying your price, always go back to the results your customers get from the work you do together. One of the callers on the radio show helps explain this concept: "I've helped people make career decisions. In one case, one person was faced with moving her family or quitting her long-term job and starting over somewhere else. I was able to help her through that. She said, 'I'm enjoying great success on a completely different career path and my family and I have never been happier'."

Let's say the caller charged $300 for the session to help her client make this important career decision. If her customer didn't employ her services and made the move, how much would it have cost them if it was not the right choice? It could be as much as

$300,000–a thousand times more than the session! I hope this helps you understand that nothing is either expensive or cheap in itself. Something can be expensive or cheap only compared to the value of the results. If someone says their session is $300, that is not expensive if it can prevent a mistake that could cost a thousand times more. It is worth it if it could also help avoid the upset and heartache that can result from a mistake like this.

It is hard to talk about money when you are in your ego and fears show up. If this happens to you, just breathe through it. As you gain more experience and as you work through the exercises to transcend your ego and fears, it will become easier.

Talking about prices in person gives you the opportunity to discuss them with your potential client. When you are in person, you can discuss all of the factors related to the decision of whether to engage your services or not. It gives your potential client the opportunity to assess the risks and make a decision that is right for them. They might still choose not to invest in working with you and that is okay. They have the right to their choice. All you need to know is that you have done your best to support them in making the right decision.

Setting Up Your Prices in a Way that Allows You to Thrive

To really know if you have set your prices right, you need to do one more calculation. This will help you figure out if you have the chance to thrive in business.

1. **Figuring out your desired income:** What is your income goal? Is your income goal for next year $25,000, $55,000, $100,000, or more? This, of course, depends where you are in your business journey. In your first year of business, $25,000 is a good achievement; second year aim for $55,000, and third year try over $100,000. These are all achievable goals if your

business is set up right. Let's say you are in the first year and your goal is $25,000. No matter what your ambition is, follow this process to check if it will work out for you.

2. **Accounting for all of your services and products:** List all of your services and products with their corresponding prices. Let's assume that you charge $80 per session and $25 for a group program.

3. **Quantifying your time:** Figure out how much time you put in to deliver each of your services or products. For example, if you do an in-person healing session that lasts one hour, you will also spend 15 minutes before to prepare and 15 minutes after to close the session. This means you spend an hour and a half for each of those sessions. Assume you also have a group program for 10 people and you spend six hours of your time to deliver that each week.

4. **Deciding how much time you want to commit:** Establish how many hours you are comfortable working each month. Let's say you work 40 hours a week, which is 160 hours a month. From this number you have to subtract about 40 percent for tasks such as decision making, marketing, sales, content creation, personal development, bookkeeping, and administration. As this is your first year, we assume you are doing all of those things yourself. If you have hired people to do those things for you, you will have more time but you will have to subtract the amount you pay for those services from your total sales. From 160 hours you are left with 96 hours, which is 24 hours per week.

Now let's do the calculations to see if you've set up your prices in a way that will allow you to thrive.

From the 24 hours per week, you can do two group programs at six hours each. This takes up 12 hours of your time. During the remaining 12 hours, you can do eight sessions at one and a half hours each.

In terms of income, you will make $500 for the group program

($25 x 10 people x 2 groups) and $640 for the one-on-one sessions ($80 x 8). This means that you can make $1,140 per week, which is $4,560 per month.

If we multiply your monthly income by 10 (instead of 12 because I'm assuming you'll be taking some vacation and time off), this gives you an annual income of $45,600. This is way more than the $25,000 that you set as your goal! Typically, it takes several years to be at full capacity. Your reality in your first year will be somewhere in the 80 percent range. Still, with this model and those prices, you can achieve your goal!

To check if you have the right prices that will allow you to thrive, figure out how many units of your product or service you have to sell a month to make your income goal while working your desired hours. Are you able to pay for your business expenses and personal expenses, and have some money left to save or to invest back in your business? This is what you need to consider in order to determine if you have set your prices right. If you cannot make a decent living from your business, you may not be able to sustain it.

Relieve Financial Pressure to Make the Sale

Hunger is the best cook, they say. Have you ever been grocery shopping when you're hungry? I always end up buying more than I need. And if I'm hungry, I don't cook. I snack on something just to feel better in the moment.

Does needing money desperately make you better at sales? No. Here's what I have found: when you are desperate, you cannot attract clients as your vibration is fearful and low. Clients are tuned in to you energetically. Everybody can feel fear and desperation, and if they do, they will stay away.

When you connect with a potential client, remind yourself that you don't need that person's money. You are there to help and if you are a fit, you will continue. If not, you are okay; you are safe.

In order to attract clients, you need to be financially stable. Here are some strategies to relieve financial pressure:

Be careful what you spend your money on

At the beginning of their business journey, many entrepreneurs invest heavily in courses, fancy websites and business cards, office space, and other items they feel are necessary for their success. My advice is to invest carefully and to check if what you want to invest in will give you an immediate return. Always ask yourself if your investment will help you earn more money.

Let's say you have Reiki Level 1 and 2, and now you want to take Level 3. If you are not practicing and seeing clients with the certifications you have already, what makes you believe that a level higher will bring you clients? I have seen this so many times with entrepreneurs. They leave the corporate world with good savings, and they take all sorts of courses and spend all their money before getting any clients. Once the savings are gone they start to feel financial pressure because they are not producing income.

Spiritual entrepreneurs invest thinking that somehow the abundance will flow. You need to have a plan of action. It is wise to spend carefully until you see some income coming in. Even when you have income coming in, if you spend more than you make, you will find yourself under financial pressure. It is simple mathematics.

Depending on your situation, you might choose organic business growth. This is when you invest a little into your business, then you make some income, and then you invest a little more and make more income and so on.

I have also seen people who infuse capital in their business at the beginning and obtain results faster. It all depends on the situation and how prone to risk you are. Employing certain tactics for business growth before your business is ready might just waste your money. Have patience, as we discussed earlier. You are in this for the long run.

Make changes to your finances

Let's say you've accumulated some debt and financial pressure is a reality for you. You need to find a way to change this. You can refinance, apply for debt consolidation, or take out some savings. If you get rid of your debt, don't take it as an invitation to spend more.

When you find yourself in debt, another strategy to reduce the pressure is to cut down your overhead expenses. We used to have an office downtown on Main Street. In the beginning, this was an advantage to attract clients. At a certain point, however, there was no longer any reason for being in an office because most of my clients were over the internet. We decided to cut overhead expenses and move our office home.

Look to see what your monthly payments are for things like rent, office supplies, and software programs, and ask yourself if those expenses make you money now. If they don't contribute to your ability to make money, you can let those things go and you can go back to them when you need to.

For example, if you don't have clients yet, don't invest in an online booking calendar even if it only costs $10 a month. Enter in your bookings manually until you become busy enough to need a solution that saves you time. New entrepreneurs are tempted to go with all the bells and whistles because they want to feel like a "real" business. Remember, you have a real business when you sell a product or service and receive money in exchange. You have a real business when you have clients.

Look at your situation realistically

Often people feel financial pressure just because they used to have a monthly income from a job and now they don't. Some people fear the worst. This is not good energy to be in. Look at your situation realistically. You may not have an income but you may have savings you can dip into for a few months. I've heard someone say they didn't have any money, and in another conversation they mentioned a $2 million investment. Look at your situation realistically.

Change your attitude towards your financial situation

Sometimes none of the strategies work. You accumulated debt that you have to pay and no relief is possible at this time. If you make the choice to continue with your business instead of taking a job, you need to change your attitude and your vibration. You have to rely on faith. Tell yourself that everything will be okay. Work on manifesting money out of the blue. With this vibration, when you show up for calls with potential clients, they will not be turned off by your desperation. You will have a chance to close the deal. If you feel you are meant to stay in your purpose and continue with your business despite the financial situation, then do so with all your conviction and dedication.

How I Stayed Committed to My Purpose-Driven Business

This is one of my most important business stories and it's about staying true to my purpose. I was about two years into my business full time, two years after I left my highly paid engineering manager job. I had joined a business mastermind and I was learning how to launch an online program. At that particular time, we had no income. I had no income and no clients lined up, and my then husband had no income because he too left engineering to open a business. One day I got a phone call from a recruiter I had connected with a year earlier. He said he had a position for me and the money was really good. He told me I was perfect for the job and they desperately needed someone to fill this position.

When he phoned me, I was in the middle of this business launch that I had high hopes for. I listened to what he said. As he described the work I heard my heart thump on my desk. It was an instant reaction. I told him I could not accept his offer because I was committed to my business. When we ended the conversation, I took a deep breath like you do when you come really close to a dangerous situation. I then continued my work for my launch.

The next day, he phoned again and asked me if I wanted to work part time. This would mean I could still work on my business. Again I said no, thank you very much. I know the work in nuclear energy; you cannot really be part time as a manger. The recruiter got upset and lectured me on how hard it is to find jobs. He told me that I would be sorry for turning down such a great opportunity.

During these calls I was fairly confident because I felt my purpose very strongly. One of my quirks is that I'm very independent. It didn't cross my mind to ask my then husband's opinion. Although he said nothing, I could feel he was upset with me. This made me wonder if I'd made a big mistake. I could have had this job; I could have relieved this financial pressure that we were in. Why did I refuse it? I must be out of my mind!

I began to feel really sick; my body had a strong reaction to this fear of having made a huge mistake. It was winter and when we arrived home from the office the house was cold. My then husband proceeded to make the fire while I collapsed in an armchair by the fireplace. I went into a deep meditation. This is one of my go-to techniques when I don't feel well. It was strange how I could go so deep into a meditation when it was cold, my then husband was making noise starting the fire, and our cat Grace was jumping on me. I usually need perfect quiet to meditate.

In my meditation, Archangel Michael took me to the Akashic records. I asked Michael to help me figure out what was best for me. Do I continue to follow my purpose and stay in my business or do I go back to corporate life so we can have money? Which one is it, I asked. I heard Michael say, "Of course, it's about following your purpose, my dear". I decided then that I would stay in my purpose and just accept that we'd be poor. We had a nice lifestyle when we were both in corporate careers and now we were struggling in comparison.

Michael told me there was no need to be poor; he said that my purpose was to learn how to make money from my purpose-driven business because this was what I will be teaching. This was the most encouraging, the most amazing insight I could have received. This gave me the energy to continue. I became determined to find a way to thrive because it was what I was going to teach.

This knowledge helped me be here today, writing this book and this chapter where we talk about prices and relieving financial pressure. Would I be writing this if I had accepted the job? I don't think so. I needed to experience every bit of hardship in the path of an entrepreneur so I had something to teach.

This story has another turn. My launch did not produce much at all in terms of income or new clients. We were in a difficult financial situation. We knew that it was time to cut the business overhead and let go of the office downtown. However, our house was under construction and we needed to finish a room to be able to move our office home. We needed some money as we were in this bind. The same week we got a phone call from my former mother-in-law. She said she was going to share a part of her inheritance from her long-passed mother with us. When she mentioned how much money she wanted to give us, it was the exact amount we needed to finish the big room and be able to move the office home!

What made her call that week, what made her want to share her inheritance with us, I'll never know. It might have been Archangel Michael giving her insight. All I know is that I understood that when I stay true to my purpose, the Universe will find a way to support me. This is what I know and this is what I teach my clients. Of course, there is work to be done to grow your business. You have to grow a thick skin to withstand rejections and have infinite patience with yourself and the process. If you follow your path, you will be supported.

CHAPTER 9

Packaging Your Services is the Loving Way to Go!

In the last chapter we talked about pricing your services right, why charging your worth is not necessarily good for business, and how to relieve financial pressure so you can make more sales.

In this chapter we'll cover another way to make sure your business thrives: creating packages. We will discuss why packaging your services is the loving way to go for both you and your clients.

Packaging Your Services is Loving for You

Peace in the world is only possible when each and every one of us feels inner peace. My name, Irina, means peace in Greek. I feel destined to influence world peace and this is why I like to teach Entrepreneur Enlightenment.

You attain inner peace when you find a way to thrive in business by making money doing what you love, and this is possible when you have learned to easily transcend your ego and your fears. Your inner peace is your contribution to world peace.

To thrive in business, you need a way to make good money in a consistent manner. You need to find ways to get out of the rollercoaster of feast and famine. Packaging your services is an important strategy to make good money consistently.

What does it mean to package your services? Packaging in general means to put a few things together and sell as a unit. For example, this technique is used in stores when they put all sorts of chocolates and heart-shaped knick knacks in a basket and sell it as a unit for Valentine's Day.

You can package several of your services and products together that your client will need in order to achieve a specific result. For example, you can put a number of one-on-one sessions, some written or video resources, and e-mail check-ins together in a package that will provide your client with the desired result.

When you sell many little things individually, it becomes time consuming and less profitable. When you put a few things together in a package and sell them as a unit, your ability to make more money increases. The setup, the billing, and the client care become more efficient. The package is a higher price and you sell all the items inside it at once. You make more money and also have more time.

When you thrive in business, you find inner peace. When you're going through feast and famine, you are worried and that's not peace.

I recommend you set up your business in a way that works for you. It needs to be aligned with who you are and how you want to live your life. If you nurture yourself and are in your flow, then your clients will be taken care of too. If you're tired, stressed, or worried, then this will affect how well your clients will be supported.

We are all different and we have different definitions of success. We value different lifestyles. If you are a morning person, schedule your sessions in the morning. If you are a night owl, it's okay to start your day later when you feel you are fully awake. Don't be shy about shifting your business to suit your style; you don't have to follow trends. Having packages helps you have the kind of business that works for you.

Packaging Your Services is Loving for Your Clients

Packaging your services is good for your clients too. We're in business to serve our customers, and we need to make sure they are fully supported.

A package provides enough time to address the core issue

Packages are a loving way to support your clients. If you give your clients a one-off session, you are only able to solve the immediate problem. There is not enough time to discover and address the core issue. As a result, you will not be able to provide sufficient support.

People seek support when they are in pain, when they are bothered by a problem and want to find a solution. When we give them a one-off session, we are helping them relieve that pain—but only temporarily. They will not be able to search for deeper answers or find the long-term solution. Giving clients a one-off session is like a headache pill: it takes away the symptom but it doesn't solve the cause. Because the cause of the problem is not solved, something else may show up a few months later that can make things worse.

Choose to work with people for longer periods of time so that you can help them find a permanent solution. When someone is searching for change or when they are in pain, they need time to explore what is going on.

My former husband used to worry when someone came to him for one session of herbalist consultation. He would give them a tincture and if they never came back he was left wondering if the tincture worked. He had no way of knowing if he helped them enough. When he switched to packages he was able to monitor their progress and adjust the tinctures to suit the needs of the client.

A package gives your clients all they need to succeed

Your clients don't always know everything they need to solve a problem. They are looking for your guidance. You have the experience of what has worked for your previous clients and you can recommend what is necessary to solve the problem for good.

You create the package by thinking about what is necessary to solve the problem and you put it together and sell it as a unit. Be a leader for your clients. Remove the guesswork for them and help them follow the path to success.

A package provides enough time to help your clients create new habits

With a package, you help clients commit to the work for months, and this gives you time to help them create new habits. If you go to the gym once to lift weights, this is not going to give you the physical condition that you are looking for. You want to go for several months so you can create muscle.

When we are left to our own devices, our good intentions wear off after a short period of time. We're busy, life gets in the way, and we forget about what we wanted to achieve. In order to feel better, we have to create a new habit and that takes time. When we have a coach, a personal trainer, a massage therapist, or a Reiki therapist who has a package and commits to support us for a long period of time, this is an incentive to continue. Be that angel for your clients.

A package allows you to support your clients through their process

When you create packages, you can support your clients through the process. This helps them tremendously by giving them the opportunity to stay engaged with the work and to make progress.

Once in a while, I employ the services of an intuitive energy healer. She only has one-off sessions. When I need one, I contact her, I book it and then we have the session. After that I'm not in contact with her for a few months until I feel the need for her services again.

There is no allowance for me to reach out to her and sometimes I feel the need. I would like to consult her when I have a dream that is related to the session or if I need clarification on a question. I would like to stay in touch and be able to get more support, but if she doesn't have a package that offers that, I cannot. This is why I have encouraged her, and everyone else, to offer packages. It provides a way for your client to be fully supported if they need to.

A package gives your client a plan for what needs to be achieved

People like to succeed, and having a plan or road map on how to achieve what they are after will support them. They will get more involved and invested in the results you are going to create together.

Your package creates this plan.

Having packages gives you time to create content that supports your clients

Because you have a longer commitment with your client, it helps you stay focused on creating content and serving them effectively. Your client may present you with some questions that you don't know the answer to. Because you have a package, you can take the time to research and find a solution.

It's much better for everyone when you focus on your expertise. When selling packages, you don't have to constantly worry about where the next client is coming from and with the extra time you can create more content.

A package allows your client to get outstanding results and provide testimonials

The biggest benefit to packaging your services is that it allows your client to get outstanding results through the work you are doing together. You cannot achieve this in just an hour. Working with someone for several months can make a big impact in their life. This also makes it easier for you to promote you work and the results you provide.

How can I say that someone is going to thrive in business after only having a one-hour session with me? Impossible! In my experience, it takes about three years for someone to go from zero to a thriving business. The first year is about transitioning from a previous job or another business into the purpose-driven business. This is the time when they align with their purpose and find that unique offering to bring to the world. In the second year, their business grows roots. This is the time to develop a way to create consistent business—a business that is self-sustainable. The third year is to expand, to grow beyond their limits. This is when they hire a team, form strategic alliances, and work with other people.

Setting Up Your Packages

I received an email from a client asking how to set up her packages. Let's use it as an example and do the exercise together.

Sherry Anne: I am a coach working with women in transition. What would you say a minimum number of sessions should be in a package? What is an ideal number of packages to offer?

Think about the ideal length of time that you would need to work with a client to be able to provide the results you are saying you are providing.

I recommend having three types of packages: a big one, a medium one, and a little one. The answer to the question about the minimum number of sessions will become evident after we talk about the three packages.

Packages usually have names that make it easy to understand their hierarchy, like Bronze, Silver and Gold. This example follows the Olympic Games' medals, where Gold is first place, Silver is second place, and Bronze is third place. You can give your packages any names you want. The best names are when your client can easily understand the differences between the packages.

The Big Package

Let's call this our Gold package. It is designed for someone who comes to you and says, "This is my money! Take it, I'm yours. Help me with my problem; I'll do anything to get the results I'm after. I want it fast and I want your help as much as possible. I want you to hold my hand." This person is fully committed and money is not an issue. They want your help, they want to get results fast, and they want to be fully supported.

The big package is where you include all that will help your client succeed. You give them everything you have that will help them: sessions, products, and support. It can even include taking them to the movies if that's what it takes to lift their spirits up. Put everything you can think of in this package. Of course, this package will be the highest price out of the three; the client gets a lot of your time and attention. This is the package where you can share all of your expertise. You can truly influence the result your client gets as you spend the most time with this client.

The Medium Package

This is the Silver package, and it is for clients who still want your support but only to a certain extent. They are more of a self-starter personality and want to do some things on their own. They are looking to get results at a slower pace.

Include the main ingredients for success in this package. Bundle in the essentials of what is needed so they get the results they are after. This package is a medium price and includes a moderate amount of your time.

The Small Package

This Bronze package is meant to be affordable and it usually consists of group work. It's where you teach your work and your processes in a group environment. People still get the same knowledge but they don't get private access to you.

The small package is not lower quality; it just has less involvement of your time which makes it possible for it to be affordable. You still include what is required for the client to get the results they are after, but it can be taught in a group setting and they will have to do most of the work on their own.

When I work with someone one-on-one, we can go deep into one problem that is specific to them. We may spend an hour on just one issue. In a group setting I can only work in shorter periods of time with someone.

As participants are getting less of your time, they also pay less. However, they still have a way to move forward and progress to where they want to be. Without having this option, it's like turning our backs on people who can use our resources to progress. Everyone has to have an option that is appropriate for them.

> *We are here to serve, and we are here to do good. We need to set up our packages in such a way that many people can benefit from our knowledge one way or another.*

When figuring out how many sessions to include in your packages, think about the minimum number you need to achieve the results. Put those in the Silver package and include a few extra in the Gold package. Your Bronze package will include the minimum number too, but they will be in a group setting.

Pricing Your Packages

This is how to price your packages: first, list everything you have included in the packages and associate a monetary value to each item. Add them all up and see what the total is. Once you get to the total, apply a discount. When people are buying more of your time at once, you can reduce your hourly rate because you save time with marketing, sales, and setup. This also becomes an incentive for your client to buy more.

Let's say someone buys a one-hour session which costs $120. However, if they buy your big package which includes 15 one-hour sessions, you can give them, for example, a 30 percent discount. This means that your hourly rate goes from the original $120 to $84. If they buy the medium package and get seven one-hour sessions, you can give a 20% discount. Here, your hourly wage becomes $96. Those are examples and this is a generic way of calculating the prices. Setting the package prices is more involved than this, because a package might contain other products and services.

When I set up my prices and establish the results, I ensure that the financial investment my client makes in the coaching program is only a small fraction of what they will get in return. Of course, I am not responsible for this. If they take little action, they will get little results. But if they take big action, they have the opportunity to achieve big results.

Figuring Out the Optimal Number of Packages to Sell

A word of caution: you need to ask yourself how many of the big packages you can sell based on how much time you actually have. Time is a finite element so you will come to a point where you cannot sell too many of the big packages because you don't have enough time to meet all of the requirements. You have to look at the time factor when you create and sell your packages.

Let's say you sell five big packages, 10 medium packages, and 25 small packages. Ask yourself: how is this going to look financially and how is this going to look from a time perspective?

You need to think about how you can honor your commitments. How can you have a business that you love and you feel nurtured by while you nurture your clients? How can you set up the packages and the prices so that everyone is happy?

Let's say you make the top package $1,000 and the medium package $900. That's not a big difference. You have to have them in such a way that there is a clear distinction between the big, medium, and small packages. For example, package prices of $1,000, $700, and $400 are more appropriate.

When you speak with your clients, give them the three options and ask which one they prefer. Don't be attached to the outcome. If they prefer the low package, it's perfectly fine. That's why you have that package. It is also there to help. Not everyone has to buy the big package.

> *You have to be the first one to buy your package. If you think it is too expensive, you will not be able to sell it to anyone else. Convince yourself that it is worth it.*

CHAPTER 10

Learning to Love Closing the Sale

In this chapter, we'll focus on closing the sale, and with this we'll conclude the discussion about money. We have talked about how to release the fears of receiving money for your services and how to price your services right. We have also explored how to package your services, how to talk about the results, and how to give your potential client enough information to help them make a decision. Now it's time to get into the details of closing the sale.

Rumi has an interesting take on enlightenment:

> *"When you do things from your soul, you feel a river moving in you, a joy."*

When our business is aligned with our purpose, we are doing things from our soul. As we do our work, we feel this river moving inside of us. It is a river of gratitude, of appreciation, of abundance, and of joy. When we do our business from our soul, whatever we put out into the world—our knowledge, our love, our care—comes back, like a river moving through us. In the process, we heal ourselves and our clients.

Eckhart Tolle says that

> *"non-resistance, non-judgment, and non-attachment are*
> *three aspects of true freedom and enlightened living."*

This relates directly to closing the sale.

When you show up to the sales call with no resistance to the sales process, no judgement towards your potential client, and no attachment to what decision they are going to make, you have mastered the process.

The Necessity of Closing the Sale

You can have the best service or product, but if you are not selling it, you cannot help anyone. If you don't help anyone, you cannot live your purpose.

Your purpose is to share love through what you know, your skills, and your business. If you want to make the world a better place, then you need to have people use your service or product. This means you need to learn how to close the sale.

Therefore, if you love your clients, then you've got to love closing the sale and initiate the money talk.

Why Spiritual Marketing is Not Enough

Spiritual entrepreneurs like to rely on spiritual marketing and spiritual sales. This is when we pray and ask for guidance: if this person is meant to work with me, let them know. This is when we pray that the right people find us at the right time. As an example, here is a prayer from one of my intuitive healers: please send me people who will be blessed by my services.

The questions that I hear from spiritual business owners are:

> Is it good to influence someone's free will?
> If I intend to make the sale and I'm insistent, is that spiritual or self-serving and ego-based?
> Is it authentic to promise results that I cannot guarantee?

Spiritual marketing and spiritual sales would work if both the person who is selling and the person who is buying are in an enlightened state. Someone is in an enlightened state when they have transcended their ego and fears; they know they have an important purpose and are determined to fulfill it. If you are in an enlightened state and your potential customer is in an enlightened state, and both of you listen to the guidance you receive, then yes, spiritual marketing and spiritual sales work.

Transcend Your Ego and Fears to Close the Sale

Unfortunately, when the sales conversation happens, both the seller and the buyer are influenced by their egos and their fears.

For you, the seller, you fear rejection if the buyer says no. You may also subconsciously fear the buyer saying yes and accepting your offer. In this case, you worry about what would happen if they don't find your service or product good enough.

To transcend your fears, you need to do the work we discussed: you need to know what you are offering and why, you need to know the results people get from your services and products, and you need to know the basis for your prices. This will help you stay in an enlightened state.

The potential client, or the buyer, can have many fears show up too. They might feel uncomfortable knowing that they are in a sale conversation, and could be apprehensive about possibly having to reject you. In general, people like to please others because of their need for acceptance. If they have to say no, they might feel guilty for upsetting and rejecting you.

If they want to say yes, the fear of making the wrong decision shows up. They may think about what your service or product means for them, and whether it will help them solve their problem. They may be concerned with what other people will think of them for purchasing your offer. They will have an internal chatter and might be distracted by it.

When you feel that your potential client is tense, you might be tempted to end the call fast, give up, and run away. Don't! Understand their fears and help them overcome them.

When you are selling, you are, in fact, presenting them with an opportunity to improve their life, their health, or their business. Be sure to have their best interest at heart and be kind enough to present your offer well. Remember, it's your duty to close the sale.

Help Your Potential Client Overcome Their Fears

After you've dealt with your own fears as a seller, you have to help your potential client deal with theirs. For this, you need to learn how to be assertive.

Being assertive is the middle ground between the extremes of being passive or being aggressive.

A passive person takes very little or no action. For example, a passive person at a trade show will have their fliers laid out on a table; they won't pick them up and hand them out to people who pass by. If someone picks one up, that's fine. If not, that's fine with them too.

At the other end of the spectrum is the aggressive approach. This is what most people are afraid of because this comes from the history of the used-car salesman. People are afraid of being perceived as pushy or manipulative.

When you are assertive, you tell your potential client about what you have to offer without demanding that they buy from you. You present your offer clearly, explaining what you do and how you can help them. You stay in that space of possibility, sharing your solution to the client's problem. You give them the space to say yes or no.

When you want to make the sale badly and you are only prepared for the "yes", you fear that your ego will be bruised from rejection. This, in turn, creates pressure underneath and the potential client feels pushed. Even if you're not aggressive verbally, you can be aggressive energetically because the other person doesn't feel that they have the space to make their choice.

Staying assertive without being passive or aggressive is an art. It's easier to be assertive when you are unattached to the result. Not being attached to the result means that you do want to help, but you recognize that people have free will and they may not be ready to move forward.

Learn to Be Unattached to the Result

One of the biggest mistakes I've made was to want to help people against their will. Growing up around my parents who were suffering greatly, I always had the desire to alleviate suffering in others. When I saw a person suffering, I wanted to help them, to show them another way. When I saw people feeling victimized, I wanted to show them that they had the power to control their destiny. But if the person was not in a place where they wanted to be helped, then my attempt came across as aggressive.

At that time, I was attached to the result. I felt it was important for me to help this person because it made me feel good to see them happy and it made me feel bad if they were suffering and I could not do anything to help. I have gained a lot of wisdom since. Now I know that I cannot help someone if they don't want to be helped. I also know that people make choices and they may have decided that suffering is useful to them somehow. People have free will and I have learned to respect that.

You need to be aware of this in a sales conversation. You may clearly see that your solution can help the potential client, but if they are not ready to solve their problem, then there is nothing you can do in the moment. All you can do is keep following up with them to see if they are ready.

When you are not attached to the outcome; you don't feel good or bad depending on the result. Even if you did not close the sale, you can pat yourself on the back knowing you did a good job understanding their problem and presenting your solution. Be happy that you made your offer and that now they have the necessary information. Anytime you connect with a potential client, regardless of whether they buy or not, there is something positive that comes out of it. You gain more experience and they open a bit more to the possibility of having their problem solved.

To stay detached from the outcome you need to know you are in a financially stable position. We discussed this in a previous chapter: you can eliminate financial pressure or you can change your attitude towards your financial needs. This is hard when you are at the beginning of your business and you don't have many clients. Maybe you have invested a lot of money to start up and it is important for you to make the sale because you need to eat or put gas in the car. Or maybe someone in your family is pointing fingers at you, telling you that you are in your la-la land and you want to prove you can make money with your business. When you feel pressure to sell, let it go because coming into a sales conversation with that pressure is not conducive to good results. It might actually detract from your efforts and you might not make the sale.

Remind yourself of this mantra before you make each sale:

I don't need this person's money. I am here to help and if we are a fit, we will continue. If not, I am okay. I am safe.

Yes, you need money and you want to grow your business, but it's important to realize that you don't need this particular person's money. You are not going to grab their money. Your energy during the close needs to be composed, knowing that you are safe whether or not this potential client decides to buy.

If you think like this, then you don't feel as though you're putting your hand in their wallet and taking out their money. Of course, it will be nice to make a sale, but it is not necessary. If you can have this energy, it will be much easier to be detached. Also, you will not question whether you closed the sale against someone's free will. I think it's good if your client wants to close this deal as much as you do.

Do you see why the balance is difficult? On one hand, you want to be detached from the result, and on the other hand you want to be good at closing the sale because you want to share your gifts. It is a dance. It is something that you're going to learn in time. At first, just go for it. Closing the sale will teach you more than not making any sale. If you need to err, then err on the side of being aggressive. At least that way you will have a business and the opportunity to serve and to learn.

Preparing for the Sales Call

Before the sales call, take a few breaths to ground and center yourself. Check to see if you have any fears or apprehension about the call. Say a few affirmations to release hidden fears, such as: "Let me be centered in love", "I'm not attached to the result", "I am safe; I don't need this person's money."

Have a list of questions to ask your potential client handy and also have your offer and prices ready to go. Read a testimonial or two to remind yourself of the results your clients get from you. Prepare mentally, jump up and down if you need to shift your energy, or dance to an upbeat favorite song. It's important to go on the call in a positive state. If you go with negative energy, assuming that the sale will be tough, the potential client might feel it and they won't buy. They will respond to your energy.

You can call on your potential client's soul and connect with it. Read their answers to your preparation e-mail if you sent them one. Look at their social media profiles to get a sense of who they are and what they are about. Pray for them. You can say "Let them hear their higher self-voice" and "Angels, help them know if they are meant to work with me." I sometimes pull an angel card, asking if this person is meant to work with me or what I need to know relating to the sale. Through the card that jumps out, I get an indication about what might be the greatest good for all involved.

Strategies to Overcome Your Potential Client's Excuses

There are many fears that come up for your potential client. Don't take them lightly because they are real. Don't judge them, either. We all have fears when we are thinking about making a big commitment of time or money. It's normal to have fears and to want to assess the risks.

I thought about replacing the word "excuses" in the title with the word "objections". I decided to keep "excuses" as you need to know that what your potential client is bringing up might have nothing to do with your product or service. It is about them and their fears, their way of handling life and opportunities.

To reduce some of those fears, be sure to give your potential client enough information about what you offer in advance of the call. Send them something to read while keeping the discussion about the different options and prices for the sales call.

Once you've presented your offer, then you have to ask for the sale. Here are some strategies to help you navigate the excuses you may hear.

I cannot afford it

This is the most common reason why people don't buy something. They tell themselves they cannot afford it. Do you use this excuse? I hope not. There is sufficient abundance in the Universe. It is possible that you do not buy something because it's not in your budget or you don't feel it is the right time for you to invest. Stating this shows that you are in control of your finances and you make the decision on what to invest in and what not to invest in.

When a potential client says that they cannot afford it, don't get deflated. I've seen many cases when someone says they don't have the money and then they turn around and buy something fancy or another product or course. Someone I worked with told me they didn't have the money to continue coaching and then in another session they mentioned their $2 million investment.

Having or not having money is relative. People will always find money for something they find of value. When they feel that they want something bad enough, they will find the money to buy it.

Your job then is to present your service or product as something desirable for them to have and to explain the return on their investment.

This might be easier when what you do is directly related to the potential for people to earn more money. For example, when someone pays for the full year for the Entrepreneur Enlightenment Academy, if they already have a business and they do the work, they can see a return on investment as quickly as four months. Over the course of a few years, their return will be hundreds of times more. What they learn will stay with them their whole life.

Even if you sell services such as energy healing, nutrition, or life coaching, you can still translate that into some sort of return on investment. Maybe what you do saves them money or time, maybe it reduces their stress levels so they can perform better in their job, or maybe your service helps them have a better relationship with someone. Whatever your services or products are, find the link to something tangible and explain their return on investment. Remember this:

> *It is not your client's job to recognize your value or the value of your service. It's your job to own your value, to know the value of your service, and to help your client see the value they receive in exchange for their investment.*

I have to talk with my partner

This is another excuse people come up with so they don't have to make the decision on the spot. They want to get off the hook by saying they have to talk with someone else, a spouse or a business partner perhaps. This is normal in cases where the investment is considerable. Again, don't get deflated. Your job is to know if the person in front of you has already made their decision. You need to support them and help them present their decision to their partner in a way where commitment happens.

Ask them directly if they have made their decision. Next, find out what they think their partner will say. When you ask this question, it is not to put pressure on them. It's so you can coach them on what to say to their partner.

Sometimes people have a hard time giving themselves permission to hire support and they deflect the decision to their partner. They might go to their partner with a low negative energy asking something to the effect of "Is it true that I shouldn't do this?" Maybe they secretly hope that their partner will be encouraging and supportive of them and tell them to go ahead. However, because of their low energy their partner may just agree with them. As a result, they may make up a story in their head about how they wanted to improve their life or business but their partner was not supportive.

When people are afraid to undertake something that can change their life, they want someone else to make the decision for them. In fact, they are projecting their fears onto their partner so they don't feel regret or guilt. They don't want the responsibility of making a difficult decision. Ask them what they think their partner will say, and help them have that conversation.

I encourage people to be their own authority figure. If you're going to go to someone else and let them make the decision for you, then you are not the authority in your own life. In my coaching, I find this excuse funny because those are the very people who could use my services. I have learned to stay grounded and centered to help them through that conversation.

It's fair for someone to decide they cannot do this, they don't want to do this, it's not in their budget, or it's not something that they feel they can invest their energy in right now. But when you see someone in fear trying to escape in a way that is not helpful for them, support them. If they can use your service, and you know that your service will make their life better, then it's a loving act if you can be on their side and help them make the right decision.

It's not the right time

Another way for people to get out of the sales conversation is to say that the timing isn't quite right. Again, don't walk away from this conversation. I have made this mistake a few times. Someone told me that they were enrolled in another course and that it finished in three months, so it was not the right time for them to use my services. I made the mistake of walking away, thinking I would follow up with them in three months. However, when I checked with this person they committed to something else in the mean time and again, it was not the right time.

If they have the desire and energy to work with you, and if your service or product can support them, then don't let the time excuse get in the way. The decision can still be made in the moment, and they can start working with you when the time is right. Be careful about how you let people off the hook. This is not aggression; this is assertiveness. People lie to themselves sometimes. Being on their side and helping them make the right decision is loving and supportive.

Sadly, I have met people who spent enormous amounts of money taking course after course and still not having started their business. My goal is to help people implement what they learn and help them make money so they can stay committed to their purpose. I want to save people from feeling insecure and delaying doing what they are meant to do. I want to boost their confidence and teach them strategies to be successful. I know you have your goals for your clients as well. Be firm and help them decide to improve, to grow, and to progress.

Asking for a Decision on the Spot

Many entrepreneurs worry if asking for a decision right away is too aggressive. It's not.

The perfect time to ask for a decision is when you talk with your potential client. After you have explained your packages, you are in the right energy. The emotion and the connection is the strongest it will be. This is why it is important to prepare your potential client in advance of the sales conversation so they can actually make a decision during the call.

The more time passes after the call, the less likely they are to make the decision. This is because people have busy lives and short attention spans. The energy of the connection decreases with time and they will not feel the desire to engage with you after too much time has passed.

Once you feel they are meant to work with you, your energies are aligned, and you know with certainty that you can help them, then it is fair to ask for a decision on the spot. You have a duty to ask.

Asking for Money

When someone says they want to buy your service, you then have to ask them for money. Inexperienced entrepreneurs have a tendency to get excited when someone says yes to their offer. They think the sale is done and let them go. Then what happens? They wait for the payment and sometimes the payment does not come through.

You can be happy to have a new client only after you receive the payment. When someone says they want to work with you, your next question needs to be "how would you like to pay for this?"

In response they will ask you what type of payment you take. Depending on your setup you can tell them e-transfer, checks, cash, PayPal, Square, credit card, or whatever else you have. They will agree on a certain method and if it is credit card then you take the number right then and there.

Some people get surprised when they hear that question. If they ask you whether they have to pay right away, always say yes. This is important because when people pay, the energy shifts.

If someone says yes, but has not yet paid, they are not your client yet. You cannot do the happy dance yet. You only have a new client when money is in your bank. And only then can you start the work for or with this client. To avoid disappointment, don't do any work before you get paid.

For events, people often ask whether they can pay at the door. Tell them that you need the payment in advance. In my case, when I'm teaching at an event, I'm in a different energy. I don't like to deal with money and payments at that time.

Another important thing for me is that when someone commits by paying, we get connected energetically. I can sense their energy and then I know what to teach to help them.

Paying at the door for me is a big no-no. Sometimes people find strange excuses not to come to an event if they haven't paid for it. Maybe they feel lazy or their cat threw up—whatever it is, they may just have an excuse. This is not fair to you as you've prepared for them. You've already booked a venue, printed their materials, and ordered some snacks. You've done your part.

I find it much more respectful of your time and energy when people who want to work with you pay for your service first. Then you book their appointment in your calendar, and you can start preparing for them. No need to be shy; ask for the money.

When people say yes to changing their life, whether it be their health, their business, or their relationships, and they pay, miracles happen because the Universe hears their commitment. One of my clients paid in full for the Entrepreneur Enlightenment Academy and she told me that was the biggest investment she had ever made for her personal and professional development. Actually, she said later she had never made an investment like that before. We were to meet for her first session two weeks after she booked. Just before we met, she received a check in the mail in the same amount of her payment. It was from a business deal she had in the works. It's amazing to witness those types of miracles. It's a confirmation that when a person commits, the Universe also commits to them. During our work together, she made her sales quota in four months, compared to nine months the year before. She had the investment coming back to her in more than one way.

I truly believe it is a loving gesture to make the sale. To be assertive and to guide the client to make the right decision for them is an act of love. Have confidence in yourself, have confidence in your services, and then influence your client to make the best decision for them. Of course, if they are not meant to work with you and you feel they are not aligned, then that is fine. Let them go. But if you feel that someone can really use your service, be the best that you can be and close the sale.

Gray's Story

Here is a sad story when I did not make the sale I wish I'd made. I write it as an inspiration for you and for me so that we can be empowered to sell people into the possibility of a better life.

This is Gray's story. He was a man in his early 60's and he had recently moved to the area where my office used to be. He moved because he had gotten a new job. His last job was very stressful, and the new job was becoming similarly stressful. I met him in my first month of business. We connected at a networking event after which I sent a follow-up message that he responded to.

We met informally at my office and I found out that he was looking for some more balance and enjoyment in life. He was a high achiever looking to reduce the time at work and increase his feeling of fulfillment. I went to see him at his office to have the intake coaching session and offer him my coaching services. He had an important role at a government office. I was intimidated. I felt as if I was at an interview. I had no knowledge of most of what is now written in this book. We did not even discuss the offer or the prices because I had no package. I went back to my office and I sent him a proposal. I still have it to this day.

This is what I recorded in my notes that day. This is what Gray wanted: "More time to reflect on the meaning of life; reduced stress. A good work/life balance to spend time at the cottage, to rest and play, to travel in Canada and abroad, to enjoy gardening and growing beautiful roses, to have more time for the kids, and to be available to enjoy grandkids, to enjoy parachuting and being around fast planes, to achieve childhood dream of playing saxophone, to do another model ship, fly fishing, and relaxing in nature." This is how I ended my message: "Are you ready to live life fully? Are you ready to grow, to do things you enjoy, and to explore the purpose of it all?"

He wasn't. He was too busy working, proving himself to faceless committees. He also said he did not have the money because of his son's wedding and his own house projects. He was in a well-paying job though.

A few months later I sent him my resume for another reason. He wrote back that he was very impressed with my experience. Here are his words: "Irina. I just read through your resume. You have an incredible background. I am honored to know you! You have tremendous value. Don't blush when I say I am totally impressed." Then he advised me to showcase my past experience to gain credibility. When I met him, he did not know about my credentials. I did not have any credibility with him at that time.

It's interesting to note that I maintained contact with him after our first encounter. I even tried to bring him on as a client a few more times. I invited him to a workshop. He called me persistent. I told him it's because I cared about him. He did attend the workshop about vision boards, but he did not sign up for coaching.

Six months later he was diagnosed with cancer, and six months after that he died. I feel sorry that he met me so early in my coaching career. With what I know now, maybe I would have been able to give him more confidence in the process and inspire him to invest in himself. There was so much life for him to live. He was passionate about so many things.

Yes, he did have money for his son's wedding but he did not stick around to see his grandkids. It is such a loss, such a shame. Whenever I am in a sales conversation, I think about Gray. Maybe if he got into the coaching program a year earlier he could have saved himself from the cancer. I will never know for sure if he would have lived longer but I know for sure that he would have had more life in the time that was available to him.

What bothered me the most is that I knew why he was suffering; there was a story from his childhood that was still holding him prisoner. He was finding his worth in his corporate title.

Gray, I am sorry for not being more assertive when we met. I was shy and intimidated. Maybe knowing that I could have saved your life would have given me more confidence and I would have asked for the sale. Maybe I was sent to you by God to save you from cancer. I did not know it and you did not know it either. Maybe your story will help others to recognize the need to get support when they feel life is becoming too overwhelming.

We never think about this, but what if later is too late? What if money has no importance after all?

This is why I don't take it lightly when someone crosses my path and expresses an interest in my work. Maybe I am the angel that has been sent to them. I want to help; I want to support. I want to be good at sales and I want you to be good too.

Remember Gray for me, and please do your best to make the sale.

CHAPTER 11

Be the Leader in Your Business

No matter what stage of business you're in, it's imperative to learn to be a leader.

If you are used to working for someone else, you'll have to transition your mentality to one where you are the boss. This is not always easy. Some people say they start their own business because they want to be their own boss, but they don't fully grasp that with this freedom comes great responsibility.

In this chapter we will discuss what it means to be a good boss, what it means to be your own boss, and what it means to be a leader. We will touch on four elements of leadership in your business: being in charge of the direction of your business, being in charge of the people working in your business, being the leader when a potential client is interested in your services or products, and being the leader with your clients.

"Enlightened leaders are able to lead themselves out of their own shadows" – Adrian McGinn

This quote is really interesting. As we work through this chapter, we'll uncover some ways you can lead yourself out of your own shadows so that you become an enlightened leader for yourself, for your business, for your potential clients, and for your current clients.

What are your shadows? They are the negative thoughts that make you believe you are not good enough to do what you do. They are the feelings of not being important, not knowing enough, and not being perfect.

1. Lead the direction of your business

A business is a business when it makes a profit. If your business makes money, then you are a good leader. If not, you will need to learn some skills from experts in the field.

Can there be such a thing as a good leader or a bad leader? A leader is someone who takes charge of a situation. It comes down to the question of whether you are a leader or a follower. If you're not taking charge of a situation, then you're not a bad leader—you're not a leader at all. When you started your business, you had to become the leader to get the business going.

Say these affirmations with me: I am the leader of my business. I am the boss. I make the rules and I know what's good for my business.

You have to be the leader of your business because you are the only person who understands the direction, the mission, and the vision of your business. You are the one who envisioned this business, who knows what it is about, and why it needs to be a certain way. When you look outside of yourself for approval because you feel unsure of your skills and expertise, you might get detoured from your vision. Research, learn, and ask advisors for input but be sure that it is you who makes the final decision. You are the leader.

I've heard of people going to their friends asking for their opinion about a business idea. If their friends who have no business knowledge give them lukewarm response or even a discouraging one, this can negatively impact the enthusiasm that would have made that business idea work.

Be careful who you ask for business advice. Do they have a

business? Are they successful? Do they have expertise in your area? Please don't take advice from people who are not ahead of you in business. It's just bad judgment. This is like asking someone who has never climbed a mountain what you should know about climbing a mountain. If you need to ask, find an expert. Before you ask others though, you can get clarity by looking at who you are, what your strengths are, what your passions are, and what you have experienced in your life. Work through the questions we covered for finding your purpose. Then meditate and ask your higher self; get some guidance from the Universe.

You are the expert at being you. Even business experts can give you wrong advice because they don't know you. What works for them might not work for you. What others think to be impossible might be attainable for you because of your determination and courage.

I paid a few thousand dollars for an extra day to be in a small group with one of my mentors and get some business advice. This mentor was known for encouraging people and seeing more greatness in them than they saw in themselves. I was hopeful. I had questions. When it was my turn and I sat in the hot seat, I shared my desire to start the Entrepreneur Enlightenment Academy. This mentor proceeded to question me about how many clients I had to date, how big my following was, and how much influence I had. My numbers were not that great. I felt like a schoolgirl being put down by the teacher for not knowing better. The mentor's conclusion was that it was too early for me to start such an academy.

The next day we left to come home. My then husband was driving and I was crying loudly in the passenger's seat. I cried for half of the seven-hour drive home. I was filled with disappointment and frustration. Then it hit me! This mentor does not know me! This mentor does not know what I have been able to do in my life. As a teenager, I believed in myself when no one else did and I succeeded against the odds. I know who I am. I came home in February and in

March I started the Entrepreneur Enlightenment Academy. I started it with just four clients, but I did start.

What is interesting to note in the story is that the mentor did exactly what I needed. By telling me that I couldn't achieve my dream, the mentor fueled my determination to succeed and increased my courage. Who knows what would have happened if the mentor said "Yes, my dear, you may". Maybe I would have sheepishly looked at the mentor and asked "are you sure?". Maybe I would not have gotten the drive and the resolve to achieve my goal. My mentor's response was exactly what I needed although it was disappointing at the time.

When you want to build something, claim that leader inside of you. You know in your bones, in your heart, what you are here to do. Just do it despite what others say or think. It's not up to them. It's up to you.

I'll tell you another story: I used to only do in-person retreats. I then had a vision that I should also do online retreats. I worked my tail off to sell the online retreat but no one bought that package. I knew in my heart and through my meditation that the online retreat was going to work someday. I asked my current clients' opinion. They thought this was not going to work as they couldn't see how I would replicate the closeness and the experiences they had when we were in person. If I was a follower, I would have given up then.

What I did instead, was to stay with the vision. I kept talking to people about it. During some of my clients' sessions, I saw that they could benefit from the online retreat. I kept my faith and in the end, I took about eight people through the first online retreat. Interestingly enough, some of those people were at the in-person retreat just a week earlier, and they still found the online version beneficial. The results from that online retreat, the healing that took place, and the feedback I got were all incredibly positive.

That was the beginning of my online retreats and now I do them all the time. It opened the possibility for people overseas to attend.

Now clients who are not able to make in-person retreats can still participate. This online offering just catapulted the Entrepreneur Enlightenment Academy to the international level that I envisioned and this is no small feat.

I invite you to do the same. If you know in your bones, in your heart, in your soul, that there is something you are here to create, don't listen to what other people say. I don't. Before starting to record the promotional videos for the online retreat, I sent out a survey. One person was enraged by my audacity to facilitate this difficult work through an online forum. They signed the survey with the name "Not-a-good-idea".

When you feel guided by the Universe to create something for this world, please stay with it. I chose to stay with many crazy ideas over the years and most of them worked out quite fine. And even if you discover later that one of your ideas was not the greatest, having done it gives you the opportunity to learn something. If you don't take action, if you don't implement something, then that is a loss. Being in business is about experimenting, it's about learning something new. Go and do what you feel you need to do without looking for approval.

Leaders find new ways of doing things. If you want to have a thriving business, you need to figure out what makes you unique. Make the effort to find out what makes you stand out. You cannot look around and compare yourself to others or do things the way others do.

As an enlightened leader, you need to get yourself out of the shadows. In this case, the shadow is the need for approval. Leaders don't need cheerleaders to know the way because they create the way. Approve of yourself, be your biggest fan and your biggest cheerleader, and you will be more than okay. You will be a leader and your business will grow.

2. Lead the people working in your business

If you want your business to thrive, it's very important to provide good leadership for the people working in your business. If you are just starting out, you may be the only employee. You need to provide leadership for yourself. There are distinct ways to lead yourself and your employees based on personality: over-achiever, laid-back or something in between.

If you are an over-achiever, always working, you need to give yourself rewards, breaks, and appreciation. Are you a good boss or the worst boss that you've ever encountered?

In my business at the beginning I had one full-time employee: me. I realized after a while that I was the most demanding, the most unappreciative boss I've ever had. One spring I made myself work seven days a week for five months in a row. I'd go to bed at one in the morning, wake up at seven, and work, work, work. On top of this, I was not happy with my performance because there were tasks left undone on my list.

Don't do this to yourself; it a terrible way to be. You don't achieve more, you actually achieve less. Be a good boss instead. I've come back to my senses after my "employee" told me she'd quit. Now I give her breaks when I take her out for walks, let her ride her bike or dance. I've learned my lesson. Without me there is no business; without me there is no purpose. The same goes for you. You've got to take care of your most valuable resource: you.

In order to see if you are a good boss to yourself, check to see if you would behave the same way if someone else worked for you. Ask yourself if you are treating this person fairly. We know that in any business there are ups and downs and there are times when we have to work overtime. If you need to work more, at least make sure you book some time off after. Give yourself rewards, breaks, and appreciation.

Appreciation is especially important. Maybe you have the same bad habit I used to have: telling myself that I could have done more than I actually did. I was generally dissatisfied with my performance. If you do, one strategy for improvement is to list all the things that you did do. This gives you a way to see that you probably have done a lot of work. Give yourself a pat on the back every once in a while; congratulate yourself for something you did well. You will have a much happier and productive employee as a result.

If you are at the other end of the spectrum, laid back, disorganized, second-guessing, procrastinating, thinking things over many times, changing your mind about what you want to do next and ending up not doing much, then you need a boss. Either you step up to be a leader or you will have to go work for someone else. If you want to be your own boss, you need to set goals and give yourself deadlines and incentives for achieving those goals.

After a year of running my business freestyle, I realized that it was important to introduce some corporate business processes. For example, you can have performance reviews for yourself and measure what you have achieved in a given period. If you are laid back, this is probably because you may not recognize the importance of your business or what you have to offer. This can also come from your shadow: fear of failure, fear of rejection, fear of bothering people if you call them with an offer, fear of the unknown.

You have to be the leader, a good boss to yourself, and help yourself succeed. Even if you enjoy leisure time, in the long term you will not feel happy and fulfilled with the results of your work. To avoid procrastinating, give yourself a project with a set deadline. Divide the project into small tasks and put those in your calendar.

If your project requires 55 hours to complete, you cannot procrastinate until the last day and expect that you will be able to do it. You need to plan and add tasks to your calendar. Work backwards. Ask this question: in order for me to finish this project by the end of the month, what do I need to do today? What do I need to finish this week? This is the basis of project management, establishing a deadline for the project and then working backwards to see what tasks need to be done, in what order, and by when.

We are motivated by progress and it's a good idea to monitor how your project is doing. You can only overcome your fears by taking action. The more you wait to do something, the harder it becomes. Be a leader and schedule tasks in your calendar. Don't let tasks float in the air because it's unlikely that they will get done. As you do the work, give yourself some incentives or some rewards for meeting the deadline or for finishing ahead of time.

You can role-play with yourself. Split yourself in two and pretend one side is the boss and one side is the worker and have a conversation. You will have fun and you will get some work done, and both the boss and the employee will be happy.

Now let's look at the case where you delegate tasks to other people. Let's say you delegate bookkeeping to an independent contractor, a bookkeeper. Because you are the leader of the business, even when you delegate things to an expert, you cannot relinquish the responsibility. You need to ensure the work is done correctly.

It's understandable that you are not a bookkeeping expert and you don't know what expense goes under which category. This is why you hire a professional. But you have to do your due diligence: you have to fact check and you have to bring yourself to the place where you can ask some intelligent questions. This is your business, your life, and your livelihood.

For some people, their business is very important. If there is no income from the business, they don't have money for food, or they cannot pay their mortgage. If the business does not produce an income for a while, they will have to ask themselves what to do next. Do they give up and get a job?

Failure can have serious ramifications. Even in the cases where there is a secondary income or savings to supplement the income, if something goes wrong it's still serious because it's you that has to deal with it.

This is not meant to scare you. It's meant to give you the perspective that you need to treat your business seriously. If your business is incorporated then it is a legal entity and it has certain obligations and rules to follow. If the business is a sole proprietorship and is in your name, it is still seen by the government as having some obligations and responsibilities and the books have to be done correctly. If you hire a bookkeeper and you delegate the tasks to them, you still have the obligation to check that things are done correctly.

A leader checks on the people they hire and gives them the tools, supervision, and training to help them succeed. When there is failure, the leader takes the blame.

Don't tell your employees to take care of something because you don't want to know about it. Don't give your power away because it might not end up well. There are several stories of movie stars or singers who left it to their business manager to oversee their money and ended up bankrupt. They did not want to know about that part of the business and it did not turn out well. Embrace the leadership role in your business as it is very important if you want to thrive.

3. Lead the potential client to the right decision

Another form of leadership in your business is about leading a potential client to make an informed decision about purchasing your services or product. This form of leadership is hard for many entrepreneurs because of the shadows and fears. Some entrepreneurs think that if a customer wants to buy from them, then they shouldn't need to be convinced. Others don't want to come off as being pushy or manipulative.

The truth is that you know way more than your potential client about how your service can support them and who your service is for. You have to explain the benefits and the results. You have to tell them why it might be good for them to invest. You have to help them see the value. You don't have to attempt to please, to prove yourself, or to impress, but you have to state the facts and what you believe to be true.

I once had a call with a potential client and her stated goal was to speak on stages. At that time, I also wanted to find more speaking engagements but I didn't know how. I was not sure if what I had to offer was the answer to what this person wanted. In the process of interviewing her, she told me about problems with her upbringing and feeling like she didn't belong anywhere. Those are things that I actually teach and I am passionate about. I am very successful in helping my clients becoming truly free of the past and resolving the family of origin trauma.

She said her budget would allow her to either go to a speaking conference to be on a stage or choose to work with me and be in my program. Because of my shadow, my fear that I didn't know enough about getting speaking gigs, I let her lean towards going to the speaking conference.

We concluded our call. As I was eating my lunch, I started feeling worried and scared for this lady. I asked myself why. It was because I've seen so many people try to build their business on shaky foundations, with festering wounds from their childhood, money blocks, and not feeling like they were good enough. With this, I know, comes self-sabotage. She could take the speaking course and be on stages, but it was unlikely that her success would be sustainable. I felt she would not be happy in the long run.

When I realized this, the worry inside of me increased. I said to myself: oh my God, what have I done? Because of that little fear I had at the beginning, I let her convince herself to go to the speaking course rather than come to the Entrepreneur Enlightenment Academy and work on her foundation. She would not be able to work on becoming truly free of the past. I know this is a must for building a successful business. I called her back and left her a voice message urging her to meditate and to reconsider. I gave her the reasons why.

Luckily, she had a strong connection with the Universe and was wise enough to say yes to the Academy. I am thankful I went back and corrected my mistake. She told me afterwards that while she was praying for support, a mutual friend sent her my website. It was the Universe that connected us. As a result of our work together, she resolved some family issues and in the first month cleared some debt with the amount superseding the entire year's Academy tuition. It would have been a shame to let my fears interfere with this divine connection.

As an enlightened leader, I need to speak up and share what I know about being patient and building a solid foundation first. I've seen people take course after course and not be able to go anywhere in business. I have worked with people who had brilliant business mentors, but they were not progressing because they had difficulty with the inner work. I know it needs to be done.

You don't need to prove yourself or impress your potential client. They are coming to you with a problem and you are there to offer your expertise and your solution. Give them space to make their choice, but they will make an informed decision if you are the leader and fully express what you know.

I hope this is a good lesson for you. If somebody comes to you and they feel that you may have a way to help them, be an enlightened leader and help them.

4. Lead your clients to success

The last part of leadership in your business is leading your clients to success. Your clients don't know the way; that's why they hired you. Be their leader.

When I am the client, I'm looking at my service provider to lead me. I once had a massage therapist who would ask me every 10 minutes if she should continue working on a spot or if she should move on. My brain was puzzled every time she asked me, because I didn't know how to answer. That frustrated me. I am a very good coach, teacher, and healer and I know what I'm doing when I am in charge. When I reach out for a service, I need to be led. I'm reaching out because there is an area of expertise that I don't have that's why I'm hiring that particular person. I'm not a massage therapist.

Please be the leader, no matter who comes to you and how important their title might be. When you are the service provider and they are the client, you lead. Your shadow may make you want to please them or prove yourself. If you need your client to evaluate your work, then you will not be in the leadership position. They will become the authority and you will be the employee.

I hired a video team for one of my retreats. Before I came on the stage they put a big bright light just in front of me. At the first break I complained about it and they removed it. When I saw the video, it had shadows and I was not pleased with the result. They said I was to blame because I asked them to remove the light. They were the experts. I did not know the consequences of removing it. I still expected a high-quality video.

As the leader, you have to love to support your clients. If they do something wrong (for lack of a better word) and you roll your eyes or judge them, then that is not leadership. If they knew how to do that thing you know so well, then they wouldn't have hired you. They needed guidance, they needed a leader, and they needed somebody to show them the way.

> *The leader observes what works and what doesn't, and helps people get results.*

Let's say you are an interior designer and your client comes to you with a pink pillow in a room that's orange. Don't roll your eyes and think your client has terrible decorating taste. Instead, find solutions and ways to support them. Don't make them feel inadequate. Move the pillow to another room and explain some color theory to them. They hired you for your expertise and if they knew what you know, they wouldn't have hired you. Help them get results while empowering them.

You don't need to prove yourself or to impress your clients. When you have the need to prove yourself, you make your client your boss. You have to observe: are you leading or is the client leading?

In coaching, the client is in charge of their life and they know what they want. As the coach, when you see they are not doing their assignments, have a word with them. They might give you excuses and say they are busy. As long as you say what you've observed and provide some tools and solutions, you have done your job. You cannot force your views into their life.

On the other hand, if you don't tell them what you have observed, you are not doing them any favors. They might not like to be called out but they might consider it and adjust their attitude or behavior. It's also possible that they might react negatively. Stay in your leadership position and say that you want to help them get results. Remind them why they signed up for this course. In the end, they should be free to do whatever they feel is good for their life.

I know it might be hard for you to confront people; it might be uncomfortable because you don't want to hurt people's feelings but it's your job as the leader.

This is another area where you need to stay detached from the results. You need to be proud of your work. You cannot think less of your worth as a practitioner, coach, or trainer when a client decides not to do the work.

To summarize, you are the leader of your business in these four areas: leading the direction of your business, leading yourself and other people who work in your business, leading potential clients to make the right decision, and leading your clients to get the results they are after. All those areas call for your leadership and power.

Be an enlightened leader. Take yourself out of your shadows, transcend your ego and your fears, and bring yourself into your power. Show people the way, show yourself the way, and lead your business to thrive.

IRINA'S ENTREPRENEUR ENLIGHTENMENT PHILOSOPHY

I've collected the main ideas from the book here so you can review them quickly whenever you need some inspiration. This is the core philosophy that will help you become an enlightened entrepreneur and thrive in business while following your purpose.

1) When you align your business with your purpose, it's easy to pursue both spiritual growth and business success.

2) Being in a state of enlightenment means you have transcended your ego and your fears, fully accepted that you are a perfect expression of the divine, and understood you came into this life with an important purpose.

3) There is a path to enlightenment through entrepreneurship.

4) When you feel that you are working hard but you're not achieving the results you expected to achieve, don't work harder. Instead, stop and ask yourself:
   - Am I working from love or ego and fear?
   - Am I more focused on my purpose or money?
   - Do I feel deserving and good enough or unworthy?
   - Am I taking chances or am I limiting myself?

> Am I aligned with my path?

> Am I allowing others to support me?

5) If you want to thrive, you need to find ways to progress that are sustainable and fulfilling. You need to find ways that give you more energy instead of leaving you depleted. This is possible only when you work in conjunction with the Universe.

6) Imagine not being able to do your purpose. Will your life lose its meaning? That's how you know you've chosen your true purpose.

7) If your purpose does not include you, it might not be your spiritual path; it might just be a fabrication of your ego.

8) If your work leaves you more tired than energized, it might not be your purpose.

9) To find your purpose, answer the following questions:
   > What are your skills, talents, and experiences?
   > What are your recurring challenges?
   > What was the most difficult thing you have had to deal with?
   > What is something your younger self would have needed to have or know?
   > What is your life about now?
   > What do you love doing?

10) Following your purpose is a real job, especially when it pays you real money.

11) When you can confidently say "this is what makes me good at what I do", people will find it easy to trust you and connect with you.

12) When you define who you are, you are also connecting more with your purpose.

13) You have the right niche when you are doing the things you love to do and have expertise in, for the people you care about the most. This is what will enable you to thrive.

14) Defining your niche helps you to focus your marketing efforts. The majority of people you serve will be in your niche. However, if someone comes to you with a problem you know you can solve and you feel a connection with them, then serve them.

15) Your potential client is mainly interested in the results they will get, not in your method or the process you use to attain those results.

16) Sharing your story is an integral part of your marketing material because it helps your potential customer connect with you. The story you need to share is the deep story of the struggles you had to overcome to get to do what you do.

17) The critical elements of a website that connect with the heart of your potential client are:
   ➤ Your relevant and deep story
   ➤ The results your work provides
   ➤ Testimonials from your clients
   ➤ Photos of you and your work

18) Build your business as you build a house. You first need a solid foundation before you put up the walls and ceiling.

19) Don't give away free sessions unless you have a strategy. Free sessions are used to grow your business, not as a way to avoid taking payment.

20) Nobody is your potential client until they tell you they have a problem *and* they want help solving it.

21) You are in your purpose-driven business for the long run, have patience. Stay true to your purpose, do the work, keep the faith, and move forward.

22) Connecting with people is the magic key to marketing. It's easy to love marketing when you concentrate on the fact that it is about building relationships with your audience.

23) We can only better or heal ourselves so much on our own. At some point we need to practice our work in order to better or heal ourselves further. Our clients provide examples that allow us to go deeper and grow.

24) Don't look at what you may perceive as immediate rejection and get discouraged. Marketing is not about immediate results.

25) No matter your personality, there is a way for everyone to be successful.

26) When you are in your ego, you don't like marketing, but when you are in a state of enlightenment and your love flows freely, you embrace marketing.

27) Arrange your business in a way that works for you and in a way that is enjoyable for you.

28) To be successful in business, you've got to love yourself, love what you do, and love people:
   - ➤ Love yourself. Without you in your life there is no purpose, there is no life. Nobody needs you more than you. Always remember that you are the most valuable asset you have in your business.
   - ➤ Love what you do. Love your service and understand how it has helped you and how it has helped other people.
   - ➤ Love people. Love your current clients, love your potential clients, and share with them what you have discovered and how you can help them.

29) When we try to prove ourselves, we put pressure on the other person to approve of us. This makes them distance themselves energetically.

30) If you don't like sales, it's because of your fears: fear that you are not worthy, fear that you don't matter, fear of not being able to deliver on the promise, and fear that the person who gives you money will have authority over you.

31) Don't charge your worth, it's priceless and then your prices will be way too high. How you establish your service price is a business decision. It's a positioning strategy and it has to fit with the clients you want to attract and the value they get as a result.

32) You have to be very comfortable with the price to make the sale with ease. When you convey the price of your service, your energy has to show that you know you are providing a

good value. The first person who needs to buy your service is you.

33) It is not your client's job to recognize your value. It is your job to own your value and to help your client see the value they are receiving in exchange for their investment.

34) Spiritual entrepreneurs have difficulty charging for their services because they feel they charge for love and that should be free. It is. You charge your clients for your skill, your knowledge, and your experience. You are not charging for love. Love is free and is on top of everything else you offer.

35) When you are desperate for money, you cannot attract clients as your vibration is fearful and low.

36) When you connect with a potential client, remind yourself that you don't need that person's money. You are there to help and if you are a fit, you will continue. If not, you are okay; you are safe.

37) When you thrive in business, you find inner peace. When you're going through feast and famine, you are worried, and that's not peace. Find a way to be at peace.

38) When defining your packages, consider the ideal length of time that you would need to work with a client to be able to provide the results you say you are providing.

39) We are here to be of service to others and do good in the world. Set up your package levels in such a way that many people can benefit from your knowledge one way or another.

40) You have to be the first one who buys your package. If you think it is too expensive, you will not be able to sell it to anyone else. Convince yourself that it is worth it.

41) You can have the best service or product, but if you are not selling it, you cannot help anyone. If you don't help anyone, you cannot live your purpose. Learn to love closing the sale and the money conversation.

42) When you show up to the sales call with no resistance to the sales process, no judgment towards your potential client, and no attachment to what decision they are going to make, you have mastered the process.

43) Spiritual marketing and spiritual sales would work if both the person who is selling and the person who is buying are in an enlightened state. Closing the sale requires both you and your potential client to transcend the ego and fears.

44) People will always find money for something they find valuable *and* they feel they want or need.

45) When people pay, the energy shifts. When people pay, they say yes to changing their life and then miracles happen because the Universe hears their commitment.

46) You are the leader of your business because you are the only person who fully understands the direction, the mission, and the vision of your business. If you know in your bones, in your heart, in your soul, that there is something you are here to create, don't listen to what other people say. Just do it!

47) Are you a good boss to yourself? Check to see if you would behave the same way if someone else worked for you. Ask yourself if you are treating this person fairly.

48) Because you are the leader of your business, even when you delegate things to an expert you cannot relinquish the responsibility; you need to know that the work was done correctly. You have the ultimate responsibility.

49) A leader guides the people they hired and gives them the tools, supervision, and training to help them succeed. When there is failure, the leader takes the blame.

50) You are the leader of your business in these four areas: leading the direction of your business, leading yourself and other people who work in your business, leading potential clients to make the right decision, and leading your clients to get the results they are after.

Keep on following your path. It's not always easy, it's not always evident, it's not always perfect, but there is no better way to fulfillment and enlightenment than a purpose-driven business. Remember this:

We fail more than we succeed in business. We do not have as many people at our events as we wish. We do not have as many clients as we wish. Some people who could really use our offer are not saying yes. Some say yes but they don't use what they bought. Some use it and get good results but don't show appreciation or leave and never send referrals.

We fail more than we succeed in business and still we have to follow our purpose. In this process, we grow stronger and wiser, we become enlightened. As a result, our life has meaning.

The pressure for you to succeed is high. The desire to be of service to others and to provide for yourself will push you forward. You will learn, grow, and expand. And you will be proud of the person you have become in the process.

Peace and protection,
Irina Mihaela

ABOUT THE AUTHOR

Irina Mihaela is a practical coach to spiritual people and a spiritual teacher to practical people. Her biggest passion is to free people from the past, help them heal, and find inner peace. She founded the Entrepreneur Enlightenment™, where through coaching, curriculum, and community, entrepreneurs are supported to thrive in business while following their purpose.

Irina is a professional engineer and had an 18-year progressive corporate career in nuclear engineering prior to founding the Academy. In 2003, she won the President Award of Excellence for Leadership. Later she managed large numbers of people and complex projects, growing her department's business by 600 percent up to $7 million.

In 2011, after a few spiritual epiphanies and deep healing from the emotional, physical, and sexual abuse she suffered in her childhood, Irina left her engineering career to follow her purpose. She discovered that there is a path to enlightenment through entrepreneurship and that the ability to transcend personal history, ego, and fears is directly linked with business success.

Irina is manifesting the evolution of her Irinuca - Child Innocence Foundation to provide horse healing to abused children. She feels that this initiative will make her mission complete. Irina is looking forward to sharing stories from her memoir *"Becoming Truly Free – A Journey from Abuse to Healing and Purpose"* with the children at the foundation. She would love to give all kiddos hope that when they follow their purpose, anything is possible.

Irina is a Strategic Intervention Coach certified by Tony Robbins and Cloé Madanes, an Angel Guidance and Rainbow Energy Healing Practitioner certified by Chris Cuciurean, as well as an Angel Card Reader certified by Doreen Virtue of Hay House.

FOR ACHIEVERS WHO
WANT MORE

Congratulations on reading the book! I trust that you have applied some of the principles you learned and seen some positive outcomes. If you are anything like me, you probably want more. The book is a starting point. Being supported along the way can make a big difference. Here are some options for you:

1) You can access the free resources mentioned in this book at EntrepreneurEnlightenment.com/EE1Resources. Those will support you in applying what you've learned.

2) The next level is to go through the video course and worksheets based on this book. Send your book proof of purchase to support@entrepreneurenlightenment.com and claim the first three lessons free of charge or ask to purchase the entire course at 20% off.

3) If you are ready to take the journey all the way, if you are ready to dig really deep, if you want to get more clarity, confidence, support, and fulfillment, then I invite you to consider joining me and the community of purposeful achievers at the Entrepreneur Enlightenment Academy. You will get access to the entire curriculum for the Entrepreneur Enlightenment; the Authentic, Empowered, Connected Process; and Business Management Strategies.

The Academy program includes the curriculum with video teachings and introspective coaching questions, live Q&A coaching and healing calls, retreats in person and online, as well as mastermind and networking groups for support.

At the Entrepreneur Enlightenment Academy, we combine personal transformation, spiritual healing, and business management strategies to support all aspects of your entrepreneurial journey.

Purposeful entrepreneurs like you have a very important mission: to raise the consciousness of the planet so that love and peace prevail. Start your journey today! Request your complimentary clarity call to see if joining the Academy is something that will propel you to achieve your vision.

To book your complimentary session to see if the Academy is a fit for you, fill in the form at entrepreneurenlightenment. com/contact

I really hope some of what you read here has helped you. If it did, send me a note. I'd love to hear from you and cheer you on or support you further!

Peace and Protection,
Irina Mihaela, BSc, PEng
Business Coach & Energy Healer
EntrepreneurEnlightenment.com
Elevate Purpose, Peace, Profit

Printed in the United States
by Baker & Taylor Publisher Services